# Cyber Threats and Information Security

## Meeting the 21st Century Challenge

A Report of the CSIS Homeland Defense Project

**Authors**

**Task Force Cochairman** Arnaud de Borchgrave
**Task Force Cochairman** Frank J. Cilluffo
**Task Force Coordinator** Sharon L. Cardash
**Task Force Coauthor** Michèle M. Ledgerwood

May 2001

# About CSIS

For four decades, the Center for Strategic and International Studies (CSIS) has been dedicated to providing world leaders with strategic insights on—and policy solutions to—current and emerging global issues.

CSIS is led by John J. Hamre, formerly deputy secretary of defense, who became president and CEO in April 2000. It is guided by a board of trustees chaired by former senator Sam Nunn and consisting of prominent individuals from both the public and private sectors.

The CSIS staff of 190 researchers and support staff focus primarily on three subject areas. First, CSIS addresses the full spectrum of new challenges to national and international security. Second, it maintains resident experts on all of the world's major geographical regions. Third, it is committed to helping to develop new methods of governance for the global age; to this end, CSIS has programs on technology and public policy, international trade and finance, and energy.

Headquartered in Washington, D.C., CSIS is private, bipartisan, and tax-exempt. CSIS does not take specific policy positions; accordingly, all views expressed in this publication should be understood to be solely those of the authors.

**Library of Congress Cataloging-in-Publication Data**

Cyber threats and information security : meeting the 21st century challenge : a report of the CSIS Homeland Defense Project / authors, Arnaud de Borchgrave ... [et al.].
    p. cm.—(CSIS report)
  "A report of the CSIS Homeland Defense Project."
  ISBN 0-89206-388-2
    1. Computer security—United States.  2. Data protection—United States.  3. Computer crimes.
4. Computer networks—Security measures.    I. De Borchgrave, Arnaud. II. CSIS Homeland
Defense Project. III. Series.
  QA76.9.A25 C92 2001
  005.8—dc21
                                                           2001001207

**The CSIS Press**
Center for Strategic and International Studies
1800 K Street, N.W., Washington, D.C. 20006
Telephone: (202) 887-0200
Fax: (202) 775-3199
E-mail: books@csis.org
Web site: http://www.csis.org/

# Contents

# Acknowledgments

The authors gratefully acknowledge the contribution made by the members of the task force, those who briefed, and those organizations and corporations without whom the work could not have been accomplished. They are the Department of Defense; the Department of Justice; the General Accounting Office; the Intelligence Community Management Staff; the National Security Council; the Critical Infrastructure Assurance Office; the National Infrastructure Protection Center; ANSER; Georgetown University; the Georgia Institute of Technology; the Highlands Forum; the SANS Institute; the University of Maryland; Advanced Information Strategies, Inc.; American International Group; the Byron Group; Computer Sciences Corporation; Executive DSL; InterTech Technologies; SAIC; TRW Inc.; Verizon Communications; and the Information Technology Association of America.

The work of this task force could not have been completed without the generous financial support of the Smith Richardson Foundation, as well as the Sarah Scaife Foundation, the John M. Olin Foundation, and the Lynde and Harry Bradley Foundation.

The opinions, conclusions, and recommendations expressed or implied in this report are not necessarily the product of a task force consensus.

# CSIS Task Force on Cyber Threats of the Future

## Task Force Chairmen and Authors

Arnaud de Borchgrave
*CSIS*

Frank J. Cilluffo
*CSIS*

## Task Force Coordinator and Author

Sharon L. Cardash
*CSIS*

## Task Force Coauthor

Michèle M. Ledgerwood
*Freelance writer*

## Task Force Members

Grey Burkhart
*Department of Defense (Ret.)*

Robert Carpenter
*Advanced Information Strategies*

Guy Copeland
*Computer Sciences Corporation*

Anthony Cordesman
*CSIS*

Justin Cordesman
*InterTech Technologies*

Steve Crocker
*Executive DSL*

Ruth David
*ANSER*

Raymond Decker
*General Accounting Office*

Fred Demech
*TRW*

Dorothy Denning
*Georgetown University*

Sheila Dryden
*Department of Defense (Ret.)*

Richard O'Neill
*Highlands Forum*

Cdr. Kevin Farrell
*United States Navy*

Alan Paller
*SANS Institute*

Seymour Goodman
*Georgia Institute of Technology*

Paul Byron Pattak
*The Byron Group*

Charles Herzfeld
*Consultant*

Capt. Leslie Schaffner, USN
*Community Management Staff*

Paul Kurtz (observer)
*National Security Council*

Walter Sharp
*Attorney*

Martha Madden
*Consultant*

Lowell Thomas
*Verizon Communications*

Rodney McDaniel
*Consultant*

John Tritak (observer)
*Critical Infrastructure Assurance Office*

Mark Montgomery (observer)
*National Security Council*

Ernest Wilson
*University of Maryland*

Paul Nicholas
*General Accounting Office*

*The opinions, conclusions, and recommendations expressed or implied in this report are not necessarily the product of a task force consensus, nor do they necessarily represent the views of the organizations above.*

# Preface

Hacker wars are now a regular part of regional, religious, and ethnic conflict—from the Mideast to the Taiwan Strait. Opponents launch sophisticated sneak attacks on each other's Web sites. A group calling itself the Pakistani Hackerz Club seized the Web site of AIPAC (American Israel Public Affairs Committee) and replaced the powerful pro-Israeli lobby's home page with anti-Israeli slurs. The Pakistanis also broke into AIPAC's databases, lifted the credit card numbers of 700 powerful Jewish supporters, and then e-mailed 3,500 AIPAC members to boast about their exploit. Israeli cyber warriors have met their match with extremist groups like Hamas and Hizballah whose computer-literate youngsters have become adept at throwing "virtual" electronic stones. The Palestinian side is calling it "e-Jihad," or electronic holy war against Israel and the United States.

The e-mail address of a group of Jewish students in Germany was bombarded with more than 17,000 messages from adolf@hitler.com containing a threat to repeat the Holocaust. The murder of six million more Jews, the sender threatened, would begin on November 9—the anniversary of *Kristallnacht,* the November 9, 1938, "Night of Broken Glass" when the Nazi regime orchestrated attacks on Jews and Jewish businesses across Germany in a harbinger of the Holocaust. German cyber police conceded they were powerless to investigate because the e-mails were sent via a server in the United States, thereby falling outside the German laws that make neo-Nazi propaganda a crime. Germany has repeatedly complained that U.S. free-speech laws have crippled its efforts to stop the spread of neo-Nazi ideas via the Internet. Six years ago, the first German-language neo-Nazi Web site based in the United States was discovered. Today, there are close to 800 fascist sites aimed at Germans but based outside Germany.

Cyber attacks now arise whenever disputes occur anywhere in the world. They are part of the war of words. But can cyberterrorism and cyberwar be far behind? Two young Filipino university dropouts demonstrated with the I-Love-You bug that even rank amateurs can cause billions of dollars in damage, from shutting down a corporate system and effectively putting it out of business for a day or two to loss of proprietary data.

The United States, Russia, China, France, and Israel are developing cyber arsenals and the means to wage all-out cyberwarfare (e.g., taking down the computer-driven sinews of a modern industrialized state). Terrorist groups are also developing weapons of mass disruption. The former chief political psychologist for the Central Intelligence Agency (CIA), Dr. Jerrold Post, says "conventional terrorist groups" are increasing their reliance on information technology—IT— as computer-sophisticated youth migrate into their ranks. Aggressive loners, who are more at ease with online relationships, are also easy prey for an extremist ideology. And revenge for perceived societal wrongs is always just a few keystrokes away. If terrorism is the act of the powerless, adds Dr. Post, "mastery of the computer compensates for that sense of powerlessness." Global computer networks make it easier for the new, flexible networks like Osama bin Laden's al-Qaida to communicate in heavily encrypted secrecy and organize without building a vulnerable central headquarters.

The capacity to produce, communicate, and use information is affecting every area of national security, from the way we govern ourselves ("e-government") to the way we fight wars (IW, or information warfare), to the way transnational criminal organizations increase in size, scope, and power, to the way activists and extremists mobilize support across borders. Worms, viruses, Trojan horses, logic bombs, trap doors, denial-of-service (DOS) attacks, malicious code—all are now weapons in a new geopolitical calculus whereby the substate or nonstate or even individual actor can now aspire to leveling the playing field with the superpower. The resources necessary to conduct a cyber attack have shifted from the esoteric to the mundane since the mid-1990s. Thousands of Web sites offer sophisticated cyber weapons along with details on vulnerabilities in widely used systems and how they can be exploited, programs for cracking passwords, software packages for writing computer viruses, and scripts for disabling or breaking into computer networks.

Graham Allison, director of the Harvard Information Revolution Initiative (HIRI) and a former dean of the Kennedy School of Government, cautions, "Whether at the Justice Department in the Anti-Trust Division, or at the Federal Trade Commission and Federal Communications Division, or at the Defense Department, or at the National Security Council, not to mention Congress, the undeniable fact is that people are making policy choices about issues that they do not understand and whose consequences they cannot understand." The consequences of "self-accelerating technologies" and of unlimited bandwidth in human interaction are impossible to predict. Once electronics are worn, ingested, and implanted and once the tiny gizmo hooked on one's belt packs computing power equal to what an entire multinational corporation possesses today, the human species will be making a quantum leap into the unknown.

William H. Davidow and W. Brian Arthur, two of the most influential players in the digital revolution, believe that as everybody becomes wired up, and all kinds of disparate groups and countries become interconnected, a global monoculture, where everyone has the same wants and needs, will emerge within 15 years.

"World history is more and more a story of increasing interconnection," says Arthur:

> As the interconnections happen, governing bodies suddenly find themselves losing control. In the 1200s or so, there was no local body that could control international finances. Bankers were sending out letters of credit and financing across countries. So you see a gradual widening of government from village councils to town meetings to states in the United States, or principalities in Germany, and then nation states. Now we have an international virtual community that's gone up almost overnight. No national government can control that. What is likely to happen is some close-knit, informal group of people will start setting up [global] policies.

Davidow adds, "You've got to think about quasi-international forms of government, which are probably going to be domain specific."

The Internet confers authority on everyone, which poses a formidable challenge to governance. Internet traffic is expected to soar a thousandfold every three years, more than a millionfold in a decade. Half of U.S. households are online—a 60 percent jump since the end of 1998. The Department of Defense alone has roughly 10,000 computer systems—2,000 of which are "mission-critical"—and 1.5 million computers. The transnational nature of the challenge was demonstrated when two obscure Belgian computer scientists were chosen to provide the encryption that will protect the U.S. government's secrets for the foreseeable future. They won the "cryptology Olympics," a contest among 15 teams from across the world. (The teams had to submit algorithms to the United States National Institute of Standards and Technology, where they were scrutinized by the world's leading cryptographers).

While fearsome forecasts of cyberwarfare-induced paralysis are overstated, the gap between cyberwar and cyberterrorism is narrowing. Richard Clarke, national coordinator for security, counterterrorism, and infrastructure protection in the Clinton administration, has repeatedly warned that hostile nations are probing U.S. computer networks for ways to spark chaos if war should break out. This is not theoretical, Clarke reminds us, "it's real." The U.S. State Department has identified 130 international terrorist groups that pose an "unconventional weapons threat" (i.e., they could try to deploy such weapons). Of these, 55 have ethnic agendas; 50, religious; 20, leftwing; 5, rightwing. Michael Vatis, former director of the FBI's National Infrastructure Protection Center (NIPC) and the nation's top cyber cop, says, "We clearly need to be prepared for serious terrorist cyber attacks on critical information systems." The tools of cybercrime, according to Vatis, "are increasingly sophisticated and available to anyone who can access the Internet."

NIPC's number one priority is to investigate the state of security on the Internet. Security is now the responsibility of each company, government entity, and private institution. Companies need to get the best security in place, but they also need to work together. "We have seen a rush of products to the market with new features, and security is usually an afterthought," Vatis said at the World E–Commerce Forum in London in October 2000.

The $2 billion plan of the Clinton administration to combat cyberterrorism, fight cyberwars of the future, and enhance computer security is indicative of the new global threats facing the United States. Disruptive and destructive technologies are surging ahead so fast that governments are frequently focused on already-old technology and thus get overtaken by events. Example: In 2000, major information technology companies from Finland to Japan adopted common standards for "Bluetooth" technology, invented by Sweden's Ericsson and named after the tenth-century Viking king who united Nordic nations under one religion, that will connect almost every machine on earth with a 10-meter radio beam.

"Distributed" computing, a new methodology that harnesses the power of many machines linked together for a common purpose, will give unlimited computing power to the individual. Together with embedded, ubiquitous sensing and computing, it may cause untold disruptions and begin changing the Internet beyond recognition in the very near term. Today the Internet is site- or destination-centric, and the individual goes to a site to get information. Tomorrow's model will allow users to gather information from multiple sources. Bill Burnham, the doyen of distributed computing, believes this will slow down the race for larger servers, routers, and other network elements.

Grid computing harnesses the user to supercomputers the world over during their idle time, thus obviating the need to purchase big machines. Computer processing power will become a commodity traded on the open market irrespective of national borders.

There are 100 million machines hooked to the Internet, all of them idle a lot of the time. The SETI@Home project (for Search for Extraterrestrial Intelligence) has signed up 2 million computer owners to crunch data from radio telescopes searching the universe for signs of life. SETI now averages upward of 12 trillion calculations per day and is already the world's busiest supercomputing effort.

*Red Herring*, a leading IT magazine, believes that this "quantum leap in the ability to gather and share information will help liberate people from the structures—governments, corporations, intellectual orthodoxies—that seek to control them." Some IT visionaries conclude that the Westphalian system, based on absolute national sovereignty, which has governed international relations since 1648, will be seriously challenged. If the nation-state is indeed eroding in cyberspace, the next iteration will be an Internet governed by international accords. Tax evasion, intellectual property rights piracy, and all forms of cybercrime will accelerate the need for de facto, if not de jure, international treaties for protecting critical global infrastructures.

Ten years ago, scientists and engineers dismissed MEMS (micro-electromechanical systems), the world of the minute, and nanotechnology (the invisible), where engine parts are measured in one billionth of a meter, as "utopian nonsense." Today, some 300 postgraduate students in nanoscience and nanoengineering are studying at Berkeley, where Professor Chris Pister has already invented "Smart Dust," one-cubic-millimeter devices that contain a communications system, a power supply, and a sensor and that have interfaced with identical microscopic devices six miles away. Four-inch communications satellites, known as CubeSats, were recently unveiled in New York, while Cornell University's new W. M. Kech Program in nanobiotechnology came up with invisible devices that mimic living biological systems.

The term "exabyte" has now entered the vocabulary. One exabyte is a billion times a billion bytes—or about 20 billion copies of the contents of an average magazine. Two exabytes is the estimated amount of unique information the world now produces every year. In other words, today's technological snapshot becomes largely irrelevant tomorrow. As physics, chemistry, and biology converge, there will be more technological change in the next ten years than took place throughout the twentieth century.

Today, cybercrime is already a multibillion dollar business. At a Berlin conference of 100 Internet experts from the G-8, or Group of 8, industrialized nations in October 2000, German foreign minister Joschka Fischer reported that cybercrime losses have reached 100 billion German marks ($42.9 billion) for the eight major countries, including the United States. "And without a doubt, this is only the beginning," he added. Eighty percent of these cyber attacks originated in the United States, Canada, Japan, Australia, and Russia, according to German interior minister Otto Schily.

Almost all the Fortune 500 corporations have been victims. The apparent ease with which cyber criminals breached the security firewalls of Microsoft, the world's mightiest software company, and obtained early sight of unannounced coming products, sent alarms through the industrialized world's computer-dependent economies. If this could happen to Microsoft, then no company is safe. The FBI, called in by Microsoft, suspects Russian hackers. Whoever stole proprietary secrets at the heart of the ubiquitous Windows program can hack into any PC in the world that uses it and is connected to the Internet.

Since the end of the Cold War, Russia has become a breeding ground for computer hackers. The large number of technical colleges in Russia has spawned a generation of IT experts. FAPSI (the Russian equivalent of the National Security Agency) and organized crime groups recruit the best. In September 2000, for instance, a conference of bank fraud specialists warned that the biggest threat to banking security was from Russian hackers. In early 2000, a 25-year-old hacker in Moscow stole credit card details that were placed onto blank cards and used at automatic teller machines throughout Europe. Some 50 people were involved in the scam and managed to steal several million dollars before they were caught. But the hacker could not be brought to justice for lack of evidence.

The target of the St. Petersburg underground "khakker" (the Russified version of hacker) network is, by its own admission, "big business capitalism." The top khakker's e-mail name is Dr. Lynux. In 1997, America Online and CompuServe quit Russia because widespread use of their passwords by Dr. Lynux's gang had made business unsustainable. The Web site www.hackzone.ru gets about 3,000 hits a day, listing, among other things, 10 "idiot-proof" steps on how to beat the system.

Several St. Petersburg khakker groups coalesced—under FAPSI guidance, say NATO cyber warriors—to attack NATO and U.S. government Web sites during the 1999 bombing campaign against Serbia. These "denial-of-service" attacks drowned NATO's Web page under a tidal wave of junk e-mail. St. Petersburg's reputation as a cyber troublemaking center was born in 1994 when Vladimir Levin and his hacker cohorts broke into Citibank's global network, siphoned $12 million from the bank's branches around the world, and routed the loot to secret bank accounts in a variety of tax shelters. It was the first major cyber heist on the Internet.

Security experts say that the majority of electronic break-ins still are not identified because (1) hackers and crackers (criminal hackers) have become increasingly sophisticated in their attack modes; (2) tools to gauge the degree of intrusion often are not available; (3) many management entities still refuse to devote adequate resources to basic risk management; and (4) the FBI and other law enforcement entities are not devoting sufficient resources to training electronic sleuths. The Gartner Group estimates that only $10 million of the federal government's law enforcement budget of $17 billion is allocated to computer-crime related training, staffing, and support.

Computer attacks are still woefully underreported. Srivats Sampath, the chief executive officer of McAfee, a computer security software group, said McAfee had spotted more than 2.8 million files infected with the Love Bug virus on its North American customers' computers in October 2000. So the virus written with 50 lines of basic code by jobless Filipinos proliferated in the world's systems for several months. Scott Charney, a former chief of the Department of Justice's computer crime division and now a principal consultant at PWC, says most companies are simply unaware that "virtual" intruders have made off with their intellectual property. Federal Bureau of Investigation director Louis Freeh has testified that this is how billions of dollars in proprietary secrets have been stolen, in many cases by foreign intelligence services and rival companies abroad.

American International Group vice chairman Frank Wisner says, "All of us are facing damages and risks we never imagined. . . . A cyber war exists where skirmishes happen every minute, and full-scale blitzkriegs are launched against companies who are not even aware that they have entered the battle zone."

Cyber threats are manifold. They come from across the street or across the world. Cyber stock scams, cyber robberies, and cyber extortions are proliferating. There are no insurance policies, says Wisner, that can begin to address the threats and risks of the Internet. Insurers are seeking a new formula with government—as the insurer of last resort for digital disasters (e.g., cyberwar, cyberterrorism, and massive cyber breakdowns)—and with software, hardware, and cyber security companies to enhance security and reduce risk. The insurance industry has been collecting massive amounts of data from CIAO (Critical Infrastructure Assurance Office) and the NIPC as well as public sources but still lacks sufficient information from law enforcement, particularly the FBI, to assess risk properly.

A recent congressional scorecard that gave government agencies as a whole a D minus for systems security has spurred the Department of Defense to try to complete a common database for battling cybercrime. This will enable CERTs across DOD, the intelligence community, and the FBI to share information critical to protecting their networks against intrusions. Means will then have to be found to share sanitized versions of these occurrences with the private sector. Other ongoing efforts include the development of new technologies for monitoring networks, reporting intrusions, and improving response time.

Washington has assumed a major share of responsibility for managing earthquakes, floods, tornadoes and hurricanes. It should now do so for cyber disasters. The government relies on private networks, including the Internet, for 95 percent of its traffic. Therefore, it has a paramount role in protecting and defending the nation's civilian infrastructure and in sharing the burden of recovery. Internet security is an integral part of national security. The government is funding the development of nanotechnology with $500 million. Cyber security is now synonymous with economic growth and global free trade. It requires unprecedented levels of funding and cooperation between the public and private sectors.

The German government has called for like-minded nations to agree on common laws on Internet crime so criminals can be convicted wherever they are based; the first step, it said, is to make it technologically possible to follow the lines across computer networks to the criminal's personal computer, or PC. But the IT industry has concerns about regulation.

IT industry leaders and civil libertarians sought to delay into 2001 the completion of the Council of Europe's Convention on Cyber Crime. They argued that the provision that would require all Internet service providers (ISPs) to retain all data traveling over their networks for a period of time is "costly and prohibitive." Some say this would be technically impossible due to increasing volumes of data traffic, estimated to be up one-millionfold before the end of the first decade of the new millennium.

The Council of Europe wants to harmonize cybercrime law and make it easier to prosecute cybercriminals by increasing cooperation around the world. But article 6 of the treaty would ban possession of malicious and harmful code. Industry CIOs say this would not work because the tools used by hackers and crackers are also used by information security providers.

Civil liberties groups and ISPs worry about the FBI's "Carnivore" system, designed as a weapon to "trap and trace" criminal activity on the Internet. According to an FBI memorandum, obtained by the Electronic Privacy Information Center under a Freedom of Information Act (FOIA) request, Carnivore can "reliably capture and archive" all traffic through an ISP. Potentially, its detractors argue, the ill-named Carnivore's broad capabilities could easily scan private information about legal activities and collect data on people who are not suspects in a criminal investigation.

Each new software development gradually erodes traditional notions of privacy. Already, 60 percent of e-mail users have bought software that can read HTML mail, according to the online research firm Jupiter Media Metrix, and the percentage is expected to grow significantly in 2001. The Korean company Postel Services attaches tiny graphic files to messages about job applications routed through its servers; as soon as a recipient opens the message, Postel knows and notifies the sender. Major electronic advertising companies, such as DoubleClick and 24/7 Media, track the surfing of tens of millions of Internet users by placing an ID code number, known as a "cookie," on the computer of any first-time visitor to a Web site where a company has placed ads; each time that ID number visits any site that carries the company's ads, it is tagged and logged.

As governments and industry and civil libertarians wrestle with Internet protection, NGI (Next Generation Internet), or Internet2, is already on the near horizon. This ubiquitous, always-on broadband connection to the rest of the world will integrate daily life the world over much the way electricity transformed the world in the twentieth century.

The Internet (and NGI) privacy issue is a ticking time bomb that will either be diffused by industry providing solutions acceptable to the public or else will explode in the form of public intervention in the management of the Net.

Vint Cerf, Internet co-inventor and WorldCom's vice president for Internet architecture and technology, says, "Security is inconvenient, and our problem is going to be figuring out how much inconvenience we can all accept for the privacy and security of the NGI."

These are the broad brush strokes on the canvas of "homeland defense" imperatives. The CSIS Task Force on Cyber Threats of the Future comprised the country's leading experts on IT infrastructure protection. Their report follows.

ARNAUD DE BORCHGRAVE
*Task Force Cochairman*

# Executive Summary

The rapid and ubiquitous spread of modern information technologies has brought about considerable changes in the nature of economic transactions, social interactions, and military operations in both peacetime and war. While providing huge benefits to those with connectivity, and intangible benefits to those without, the pervasiveness of the Internet has created significant personal, organizational, and infrastructure dependencies that are not confined by national borders. The Internet has become a "backbone of backbones," a system of networks that is complex and devoid of clear parameters. The growing codependence of public and private organizations on common systems, networks, and commercial off-the-shelf (COTS) hardware and software is shifting the ownership of these infrastructures and assets. These then go into the hands of those with the most efficient research and development and production capabilities. This process makes it exceptionally difficult to determine where to draw lines of accountability and responsibility for the ensuing strategic vulnerabilities. The challenge becomes particularly important when privately owned assets are integrated into broader national security concerns.

The Internet, by its very nature, is and likely will remain an unstable, immature, and insecure technology, open to abuse and exploitation. Concurrently, globalization and the advent of the Information Age have empowered individuals, national subgroups, and non-state actors. Because hacker tools are increasingly cheap, accessible, and easy to "weaponize," disruptive attacks can be perpetrated not only by nation-states, but also by national opposition groups, ideological radicals, terrorist organizations, and individuals. In addition, "hacktivists" or representatives from small interest groups or nongovernmental organizations (NGOs) can meet and plan online for the purpose of disrupting or derailing proposed policies and negotiations.

Several sorts of threats emerge from this new environment, each with varying levels of national security concern:

- *The threat of disruption* of communication flows, economic transactions, public information campaigns, electric power grids, and political negotiations. The effects of disruptions usually will be felt purely in economic terms and thus will be of greatest concern to private-sector entities. The disruption of military communications in times of conflict presents the potential for loss of life or aborted offensive missions. The probability of this type of threat materializing is considerable, as the tools needed to create disruptive viruses and denial-of-service (DOS) attacks are rudimentary and pervasive. Many well-documented instances have occurred in the past two years, with economic consequences in the United States measured in billions of dollars.

■ *The threat of exploitation* of sensitive, proprietary, or classified information. Information theft, fraud, and cybercrime can have extremely serious effects at the personal level (e.g., identity theft), institutional level (e.g., online credit card fraud or theft of thousands of credit card numbers), and national security level (e.g., systematic probing of classified or unclassified but sensitive government systems). This threat is made all the more ominous by the difficulty of detecting these types of intrusions and compromised systems. As with disruption, the probability of occurrence is high and there have been several notable examples.

■ *The threat of manipulation* of information for political, economic, military, or trouble-making purposes. Several recent incidents of defaced Web sites in the former Yugoslavia and the Middle East, and of altered personal financial information on e-commerce sites, point to the clear potential for using the Internet as a powerful tool for manipulating information. While many instances of manipulation simply serve the cause of making a statement and can be remedied rapidly, the more dangerous instances are those that go undetected: manipulation of financial data, military information, or functional infrastructure data (such as the timing of dam releases). These types of attacks require more sophisticated tools than do disruptive incidents, but nonetheless are easily perpetrated by those with modest resources and a reasonably sophisticated grasp of the technology.

■ *The threat of destruction* of information or, potentially, of critical infrastructure components can have deleterious economic and national security consequences. Destruction of information is of particular concern because, like disruption, it can be carried out through relatively simple hacker techniques. Examples of viruses and Trojan horses are well documented. The probability of destruction of infrastructure remains lower due to better security precautions surrounding critical national assets. The possibility is real, however, and should not be dismissed.

For the reasons above, it is increasingly complicated to distinguish between a national security attack, criminal activity, and malicious but low-level disruption. In addition, it is estimated that no more than 10 percent of all attacks are detected. Perhaps of greater concern, the multiplication effect and profound interdependencies can elevate tactical attacks or threats to the strategic level. Establishing the source, nature, and severity of cyber threats in the dawn of their real potential is a complex undertaking, but one that has gained increased urgency as nations such as China and Russia write information manipulation and exploitation into their new military doctrines and plans. Understanding these distinctions and improving America's ability to provide fast and accurate assessments of the nature of the attacks and their perpetrators are a core part of the problem at hand. There are no "silver bullets." National vulnerabilities must be addressed through improved cooperation and coordination between government agencies, between government and the private sector, and between national and international bodies responsible for both prevention and response.

In the context of homeland defense, lines of defense are centered around smaller (frequently private) organizations and the individual. Nonetheless, the federal government retains its obligation to protect its citizens and assets from both foreign and domestic threats—a particularly challenging task when U.S. assets potentially lie as nodes within foreign-owned infrastructures. Security measures currently are insufficient both within government and throughout the private sector. Low-level attacks have exposed many vulnerabilities and poor security practices. The government recently received a D-minus grade in a congressional review of systems security. Of greater concern, attacks to date have been relatively benign compared with the potential offered by current technological tools. A Love Bug or Melissa virus multiplied one-hundredfold would rapidly escalate to the level of a national security crisis. In the face of this potential, it is essential that government clearly articulate a definition of the problem, a statement of its position, and a precise delineation of the chain of command in the event of a cyber attack on U.S. assets. On a more focused scale, the government must improve its internal information and personnel security practices; encourage increased information sharing with the private sector concerning vulnerabilities and solutions, particularly with respect to shared systems; and provide private-sector industries with incentives for improving their security practices.

Government can improve cooperation with the private sector in many ways:

- through information sharing on vulnerabilities, warnings of ongoing attacks or threats, information on hacker modus operandi, and solutions and defenses to established threats and attacks;

- through continued facilitation of discussions within industry sectors, interaction with information sharing and analysis centers (ISACs), and assistance in collecting, sanitizing, and disseminating pertinent warnings of threats and attacks;

- through building upon the successful elements of the National Infrastructure Protection Center (NIPC) model while learning from its mistakes (most notably, its inconsistencies in reciprocating information sharing, and its tendency to request private-sector action using national security language rather than business language); and

- through the establishment of a single point of national coordination for cyber concerns and alerts, specifically, the creation of both an office for a cyber "commander" (or "national Chief Information Officer"), and a "cyber 911" virtual center that would issue warnings, provide security-related information, and coordinate multiple-agency responses in emergencies. Unlike the NIPC, this new virtual center would not be housed within the Department of Justice, but rather within an organization less restricted by its own information protection and law enforcement mission.

Government also can provide specific incentives to the private sector to better protect its systems; suggested approaches include

- collaborating in collecting and sharing risk data and acting as the catalyst for the establishment of industrywide standards for information assurance in different business sectors;

- granting relief from specific provisions of antitrust laws to companies that share information specifically related to vulnerabilities or threats;

- establishing liability limits against disruption of service for companies using security "best practices";

- establishing clear corporate liability for disruptions to consumers (i.e., limiting consumer liability in ways similar to the Electronic Fund Transfer Act);

- providing extraordinary liability relief to the private sector in the case of cyber-warfare, similar to the indemnification authorities set up in the case of destruction of commercial assets through conventional warfare;

- providing specific awards or credits for information leading to hacker arrests; and

- enacting intermediate regulatory steps (both domestic and international) governing shared systems.

Government can also increase its credibility with the private sector by taking certain internal measures:

- generating an agreement across agencies on a clear definition of the problem and a clear delineation of responsibilities (e.g., warning vs. defense vs. prosecution);

- improving its internal security practices, including strengthening the requirements for system upgrades and timely antivirus software upgrades, tightening personal security requirements, and instituting personnel accountability for the handling of sensitive government data;

- improving information-sharing processes and incentives within and between agencies;

- establishing policies at the agency level that focus not only on remediation but also on reconstitution and continuity of operations;

- working toward altering the incentive structure in the law enforcement and intelligence communities so that prevention becomes as important as prosecution;

- vastly improving education and training not only of security professionals, but of all government employees who handle sensitive data on government information systems;

- providing direct financial incentives to universities to develop information security curricula and to integrate information security not only into their current information science programs, but into their humanities and public policy courses as well; and

- working toward more comprehensive legislation for international collaboration on both the prevention and prosecution of cyber crimes and cyber aggressions.

As new forms of technology such as open-source software, mobile code, and nanotechnology emerge and continue to increase in sophistication, the issues of authority, responsibility, and capability to counter cyber threats will be magnified both in scope and in complexity. The need for rapid reaction will continue to supersede the capability for detection, identification, and prosecution. The United States must work toward a comprehensive response policy designed to thwart all attacks on national infrastructures and assets—be they within or without U.S. borders—in order to have the necessary flexibility and preparedness to counter the cyber threats of the future. The recommendations provided above offer suggestions for first steps in that direction.

# Introduction

The rapid and ubiquitous spread of modern information technologies has brought about considerable changes in the global environment, ranging from the speed of economic transactions to the nature of social interactions to the management of military operations in both peacetime and war. Governments, academic institutions, private corporations, armed forces, and individuals now share a common, global infrastructure and benefit from increased connectivity. At the same time, the pervasiveness of the Internet has created significant personal, organizational, and infrastructural dependencies that are not confined by national borders. Even members of developed societies who do not actively seek to use the Internet in their personal or business transactions depend on its proper operation in ways not always visible to them.

The Internet permeates and ties together infrastructures, daily operations, and security structures in ways no other technology has—from databases containing the records of financial institutions to online medical records to safety features and sensor controls in elevators to home appliances such as refrigerators. The technology continues to change and insinuate itself into everyday life more rapidly than society's collective consciousness of it. For example, most cars produced in the year 2000 came equipped with Internet connections, a concept that might have been considered absurd only five years earlier. For all of these reasons, the effects of modern information technologies differ from those of new technologies before them. The Internet is a system of networks of unparalleled complexity that is amorphous, devoid of clear parameters, and ambiguous in ownership.

The growing codependence of public and private organizations on common systems, networks, and commercial off-the-shelf (COTS) hardware and software is creating new and challenging vulnerabilities, both tactical and strategic. The Internet, by its very nature, is an unstable, immature, and insecure technology, open to abuse and exploitation. As the systems used in both public and private organizations and in the management of infrastructures increasingly migrate to Web-based protocols, the potential for disruption increases. This disruption can be low-level and inconsequential on a national security scale—for example, the defacement of a personal Web site or the spread of a virus that clogs up e-mail inboxes. But the disruption can also scale up to the level of interference with military communications, significant power outages, or important economic losses due to large-scale denial-of-service (DOS) attacks—all of which have implications for national security and homeland defense. Serious disruptions already have been caused by recreational hacking, online activism ("hacktivism"), cracking, and the malicious unleashing of viruses and DOS attacks. Well-documented incidences of cybercrime—ranging from identity theft to fraud to economic espionage to cyber extortion—have become alarmingly frequent.

Establishing the source, nature, and severity of cyber threats at the dawn of their real potential is a complex undertaking. Understanding the distinctions between attacks and motives, and improving the nation's ability to provide fast and accurate assessments of the nature of both the attacks and their perpetrators, are a core part of the problem. Globalization and the advent of the Information Age have empowered individuals, national subgroups, and nonstate actors. Because the Internet is so pervasive and because hacker tools are increasingly cheap, accessible, and easy to "weaponize," threats on United States soil come not only from other nation-states, but from national opposition groups, ideological radicals, terrorist organizations, and individuals. Thus, both the likely criminal entities and the damage they seek to inflict become more difficult to identify, quantify, and warn against. It is increasingly complicated to distinguish among a national security threat, criminal activity, and malicious but low-level disruption. In addition, globalization has made it difficult for government to focus its actions on threats to international networks, as the government structure has not kept pace with the new transnational environment. Compounding the challenge is the fact that basic security practices and technologies are underutilized in both the public and private sectors.

There is no "silver bullet" solution to addressing the societal and security threats that will continue to grow as information technologies become increasingly sophisticated and transparent. As ownership of critical infrastructures moves increasingly into private hands, and as government continues to transition to COTS technology and shared networks, the space between private-sector responsibility and the need for government action gains new importance. At the heart of the domestic challenge lies the lack of alignment between authority, responsibility, and capability between the public and private sectors. Under current government structures and public-private partnerships, those with the authority to act often lack the capability, while those with the capability (and understanding) do not necessarily have a responsibility (or jurisdiction) to act.[1]

Aligning these dimensions is critical to the nation's ability to counter cyber threats. Several straightforward measures can be taken to improve security features and practices to protect individual businesses and agencies as well as critical national assets. To this end, this report provides multiple recommendations, which include the following primary suggestions for action within the U.S. government:

- Clearly articulating a definition of the problem, a statement of the U.S. position, and a precise delineation of available government resources and the chain of command in the event of a cyber attack on U.S. assets.

- Encouraging increased reciprocal information sharing with the private sector concerning vulnerabilities and solutions, particularly with respect to shared systems. Mechanisms include continued facilitation of discussions within

---

1. For a detailed analysis of these alignment challenges, see Jeffrey R. Cooper, *Towards a National Information Strategy: Aligning Responsibility, Authority, and Capability to Provide for the Common Defense* (Center for Information Strategy and Policy, Science Applications International Corporation, McLean, Va., September 1, 1999).

industry sectors, the removal of impediments to information sharing (e.g., through the creation of Freedom of Information Act, or FOIA, exemptions), and the establishment of a central point of national coordination in the form of both a "national CIO" and a virtual "cyber 911" center.

- Providing private-sector industries with incentives for improving their security practices beyond the minimum demanded by market pressures and profit concerns. These incentives range from tax breaks to relief from specific provisions of antitrust laws to the clear establishment of corporate liability, liability limits, and extraordinary liability relief provisions, with attendant insurance measures.

- Promoting and requiring dramatic improvement in internal government practices, from consistent use of basic antivirus software to more education and training of security professionals to personal accountability for sensitive information. Measures must also include improved interagency information sharing and a conscious, sophisticated public information and education campaign.

- Moving away from the current posture of passive response to a culture of planned, strategic response that will both provide the necessary preparedness and authority for agencies to act effectively in the event of a cyber attack and ensure the capacity for retribution as well as defense.

- Establishing and adjusting the legal infrastructure needed to support the prevention, remediation, or prosecution of cybercrimes, acts of cyberterrorism, or acts of information warfare, at both the domestic and the international level.

# CHAPTER 2

# The New Definition and Ownership of the National Interest

## A Broader Definition of National Security

National security in this age of globalization, post–Cold War politics, and daily information technology revolutions is no longer confined to the economic, military, and foreign policy domains. Moreover, national security concerns exist not only in the physical world, but also in the nebulous world of cyberspace. The triumph of market forces has combined with the spread of information technologies to create an entire "New Economy" where transactions are instantaneous and uninterrupted and where negotiations are often intangible or invisible. Nonetheless, transactions occurring in this medium provide the basis for productivity and growth in every sector of human endeavor. Thus it is important to distinguish different levels of national security and to acknowledge the differences between the agencies of government involved directly in addressing national defense and those responsible for law enforcement, economic matters, or social policies. A cyber threat against critical infrastructure assets or a national military will require a very different response than a spate of criminal activity targeting financial institutions. To better understand and characterize the new threats to national security, a greater degree of transparency between the many parts of government addressing the problem is critical.

The advent of the Information Age also has created new national security roles for the public and private sectors, as well as new opportunities for the empowerment of individuals, small groups, and transnational nonstate actors. As a result, threats no longer originate simply from armies or national entities. At the same time, the ownership and responsibility for maintenance and protection of national infrastructure assets such as roads and airspace, and tightly knit assets such as telephone and electrical power distribution, are more widely diversified than was the case with wholly owned government assets. The fact that infrastructure ownership continues to evolve as rapidly as infrastructure dependence presents substantial new challenges for all governments, and these are compounded by the increasing number of assets requiring government protection.

There are several recent examples of how formerly industry-specific concerns have risen—or have the potential to rise—to the level of national security concerns. Perhaps the most recent was the acknowledgment by Microsoft that hackers had broken into their systems—using a relatively unsophisticated program—and accessed next-generation Windows software that was not only unreleased but not yet even announced. Microsoft reacted quickly to this event, conducting an extensive review of their processes, including wide-ranging auditing of systems that contained Microsoft products. The message, however, is clear: if hackers can penetrate the security perimeter of the world's most powerful software company, then others certainly are not immune.

The range of potential predators targeting U.S. infrastructures and assets is significant and starts at the level of the nation-state. Countries such as China are incorporating notions of data manipulation, information exploitation, and unrestricted warfare into their emerging military plans.[2] As part of its economic reform, China is laying a countrywide, state-controlled, fiber-optic backbone. In addition, many nations have embraced the asymmetric warfare concept and are making substantial investments in their own infrastructures and capabilities. The 1999 Chinese People's Liberation Army (PLA) publication *Unrestricted Warfare* describes this strategy as follows:

> Supposing a war broke out between developed nations already possessing full information technology, and relying upon traditional methods of operation, the attacking side would generally employ the modes of great depth, wide front, high strength, and three-dimensionality to launch a campaign assault against the enemy. Their method does not go beyond satellite reconnaissance, electronic countermeasures, large-scale air attacks plus precision attacks, ground outflanking, amphibious landings, air drops behind enemy lines....[T]he result is not that the enemy nation proclaims defeat, but rather one returns with one's own spears and feathers. However, by using the combination method, a completely different scenario and game can occur: if the attacking side secretly musters large amounts of capital without the enemy nation being aware of this at all and launches a sneak attack against its financial markets, then after causing a financial crisis, buries a computer virus and hacker detachment in the opponent's computer system in advance, while at the same time carrying out a network attack against the enemy so that the civilian electricity network, traffic dispatch network, financial transaction network, telephone communications network, and mass media network are completely paralyzed, this will cause the enemy nation to fall into social panic, street riots, and a political crisis. There is finally the forceful bearing down by the army, and military means are utilized in gradual stages until the enemy is forced to sign a dishonorable peace treaty.[3]

Thus, although the United States might not readily make use of computer network attack (CNA) tactics, other countries might not show the same hesitation. Currently, at the level of national security and homeland defense, the United States

---

2. The nonpartisan Congressional Research Service (CRS) recently released a report on China's development of a strategic information warfare unit. For details, see Jason Sherman, "Report: China Developing Force to Tackle Information Warfare," *Defense News*, November 27, 2000.

3. Qiao Liang and Wang Xiangsui, *Unrestricted Warfare* (trans. FBIS) (Beijing: PLA Literature and Arts Publishing House, February 1999), p. 75.

is not adequately prepared for this possibility. At the same time, the strategic focus of the United States cannot be limited to threats from nation-states. Specifically, the focus also must be on what a terrorist organization might do to target a specific sector of the economy, such as the financial services industry or power companies. Such attacks would have international ramifications, especially as many sectors are now transnational institutions.

To date, no severe incidents of nation-based cyberwarfare have been detected. At the level of smaller actors, however, the statistics are more telling. According to Interpol, 30,000 hacker Web sites currently exist on the Internet. Between 1989 and 1999, there were only 34,000 reported global hacking incidents, but between January and October 2000 alone, 50,000 incidents were reported.[4] In 1999, the Department of Defense detected 22,144 electronic attacks against unclassified U.S. military computer systems, a threefold increase over the number detected the previous year.[5] In 2000, the number of such attacks rose roughly 10 percent, with more than 14,000 detected in the first seven months of the year alone.[6] To put these numbers in further perspective, the Computer Emergency Response Team (CERT) Coordinating Center at Carnegie Mellon University has estimated that only 10 percent of attacks are detected and that far fewer are reported.[7]

It is difficult to estimate the financial repercussions of such a volume of attacks on a global scale. Studies to date, however, point to disconcerting figures, many of which are all the more alarming because they represent conservative estimates. As the figures grow, they begin to rival statistics for bricks-and-mortar crimes such as check fraud and offline credit card fraud, currently the two most significant sources of loss at financial institutions. At a recent meeting of the Group of Eight (G-8) industrialized nations, German foreign minister Joschka Fisher noted that, within the G-8, "losses from cybercrime are at $42.9 billion a year. And without a doubt, this is only the beginning."[8]

Thus, a thorough rethinking of a national strategy to protect U.S. national interests is essential. National security must be redefined to encompass the new range of national information infrastructure interests critical to the United States. To that end, the accepted definition of national security should specifically include such elements as critical private-sector assets and critical information flows that shape public opinion and consumer confidence.

---

4. Comments by David Rose, organizer of the October 2000 World E-Commerce Forum in London. Matt MacLean, "Cybercrime threat 'real and growing,'" *BBC News Online*, Science and Technology Section, October 19, 2000.

5. Walter Pincus, "Hacker Hits on Pentagon Computers Up 10% This Year," *Washington Post*, December 9, 2000, p. A8.

6. Ibid.

7. Several papers providing statistics on attempted attacks or intrusions, as well as the percentage detected and reported, can be found at http://www.cert.org/research/. Statistics also are provided on tests run by various government agencies.

8. "Internet experts debate new tactics against cyber crime," *Reuters*, October 24, 2000.

# The New Threat Construct

Unlike certain forms of more conventional attack, or homeland defense concerns such as chemical and biological warfare, cyber attacks alone are not likely to lead to a nation's collapse. With 95 percent of U.S. military traffic moving over civilian tele-communications and computer systems, however, the United States' reliance on information systems has become a strategic vulnerability. Although the direct destructive effects of cyber attacks are on a lesser scale than those of more conventional forms of attack, cyber attacks can have severe impacts on national objectives and security interests. Because of the profound interconnectivities and interdependencies created by the Internet, attacks can easily be multiplied, copied, or modified. The focus of the attackers is not merely on perceptions or targets, but on security goals.

Disrupting national objectives does not require as much time or as many actors as it once did. The impacts are not only more complex, but also more pervasive. The destruction of an individual target (such as the recent attack on the USS *Cole*) is a tragedy; the destruction of targets in aggregate—be they embassies, dams, or power grids—becomes a direct threat to national security. From a homeland defense perspective, there is a low probability of a single point of failure (a strategic vulnerability). Of greater concern are coordinated and repeated multiple points of failure that can cause significant disruption. The multiplication effect empowered by the Internet can cause what would normally be considered a tactical attack to escalate rapidly to the level of the strategic. At the same time, the United States Armed Forces cannot defend the nation against such attacks. Lines of defense and accountability often lie in the hands of individuals and smaller organizations.

While organized crime, terrorist bomb squads, assassins, and chemical and biological attacks are still very much at the forefront of national security concerns, an emergent class of less tangible, unconventional threats is gradually making its way onto defense and intelligence watch lists. Most notably, threats emanating from the convergence of multiple technologies and sciences (e.g., information technology, nanotechnology, biotechnology, robotics, and microelectromechanical systems) present tremendous potential for severe damage and disruption to critical infra-structures and national assets. Yet such threats are poorly understood by those responsible for their prevention. While many experts contend that serious threats—the kind that would perpetuate damage on the scale of conventional attacks—will not manifest themselves on the immediate horizon, there is nonetheless an imperative to focus on concrete preventive measures. When viruses occur that are more sophisticated and malicious than those sustained in recent months, there will be little time for rational analysis and preparation. Advance contingency planning is critical.

Setting up preventive measures and contingency plans is challenging, particularly as the effects and potential impacts of information attacks are still being evaluated. The effects of a missile attack are known and the damage is quantifiable. But forecasting the damage wrought by the stealing of information, interruption of service, and destruction of data requires methodologies very different from those established to assess damage from conventional attacks. Until "real" cyber incidents occur—those inflicting physical, emotional, or economic loss on the scale of conventional attacks—it will be difficult to predict the true damage caused by such attacks or (from the perpetrator's perspective) the success of proposed attacks.

Compounding the challenge of anticipating and planning for threats to national infrastructures is the issue of the attacker's motivation. While some cyber attacks are indeed national security threats, others merely emanate from cyber thrill-seekers. The May 2000 "Love Bug,"[9] unleashed by two junior college dropouts in the Philippines, cost several billion dollars in lost business and information and permanently damaged files and data. The underlying motivation, though, was not economic gain but braggadocio that had political repercussions.

Several sorts of threats emerge from this new environment, each with varying levels of national security concern:

■  *The threat of disruption* of communication flows, economic transactions, public information campaigns, electrical power grids, political negotiations, water distribution, and other components of the national infrastructure. The effects of disruptions usually will be felt purely in economic terms and thus will be of greatest concern to private-sector entities. But the disruption of military communications in times of conflict presents the potential for loss of life or aborted military missions. The probability of this type of threat materializing is considerable, as the tools needed to create disruptive viruses and denial-of-service attacks are already pervasive and constantly being improved.

■  *The threat of exploitation* of sensitive, proprietary, or classified information. Information theft, fraud, and cybercrime can have serious effects. From identity theft to online credit card fraud to the systemic probing of government systems, exploitation can have an impact on anyone, from individuals to corporate entities to the guardians of U.S. national security. The threat is made all the more ominous by the difficulty in detecting these types of intrusions and compromised systems. As with disruption, the probability of occurrence is high and there have been several notable examples in recent months. These types of attacks most often are sporadic, isolated, and motivated by the desire for personal financial gain or the desire to expose certain systems as insecure. Exploitation also can be systematic and state-sponsored. For example, an ongoing series of structured, persistent, purposeful probes into university, government, and private-sector systems in the United States, allegedly originating in Russia, was detected in 1999. This operation—code-named Moonlight Maze—had been ongoing for a year before being detected. While the systems themselves have not been damaged, the attackers have stolen considerable amounts of unclassified but sensitive information. Attacks continued through 2000, emanating from different parts of the former Soviet Union. Moscow has

---

9.  The most common variant of the virus known as the Love Bug is the VBS.LoveLetter.A worm. Symantec, a world leader in antivirus technology, notes that this worm sends itself to e-mail addresses in the Microsoft Outlook address book and also spreads itself into Internet chatrooms via mIRC. It overwrites files with certain extension types and replaces them with the source code of the worm, thus destroying the original contents. It also tries to download a password-stealing Trojan horse program from a Web site.

denied any involvement. The attacks have not been disruptive, but they are dangerous in aggregate. Their presumed origin also elevates the threat they pose.[10]

- *The threat of manipulation* of information for political, economic, or military purposes, or for bragging rights. Several recent incidents of defaced Web sites in the former Yugoslavia and the Middle East, and of altered personal financial information on e-commerce sites, point to the clear potential for using the Internet as a powerful tool for information manipulation. Manipulation also can occur in combination with disruption or exploitation. In a recent attack, members of the pro-Palestinian "Pakistani Hackerz Club" not only defaced the Web site of the American Israel Public Affairs Committee (AIPAC); they also downloaded 3,500 e-mail addresses to which they sent anti-Israeli messages, and 700 credit card numbers belonging to members who had made donations to the organization, which they promptly published on the Internet.[11] While many instances of manipulation simply serve the cause of making a statement and can be remedied rapidly, the more dangerous instances are those that go undetected: manipulation of financial data, military information, healthcare information, or infrastructure data.

- *The threat of destruction* of information or its underpinning infrastructure components. Destruction of information or its underlying components can have deleterious consequences for the economy and national security. Sophisticated attacks against highly specific power distribution and fuel manufacturing infrastructure targets in Serbia demonstrated the efficacy of such attacks. Destruction of information is of particular concern because it can be carried out through relatively simple hacker techniques. Examples are well documented. The Love Bug virus not only clogged e-mail boxes and stole passwords; it also caused files to be deleted from hard drives. The probability of major destruction of infrastructure remains low due to better security precautions surrounding critical national assets. However, the possibility is real and should not be dismissed.

Addressing Information Age threats is gradually becoming a more central facet of homeland defense concerns and strategies. Attacks from nation-states are difficult to distinguish from those launched by nonstate actors, who in turn are hard to identify, hedge against, or apprehend. For example, transnational pseudo-religious groups are evolving with a more sophisticated generation of IT users from physical to electronic terrorism. A national security strategy addressing cyber concerns also must focus on domestic threats, as "insiders" remain the leading perpetrators of all cyber incidents. Psychological and human factors analysis is already being undertaken by defense and intelligence agencies to address this issue, but the results are not yet conclusive. The problem is complicated by the recent trend of increased outsourcing of IT-related work, frequently to locations outside the United States, or

---

10. These attacks were originally code-named "Moonlight Maze," but have been given a new, classified moniker.

11. John Schwartz, "Hacker Defaces Pro-Israel Web Site," *New York Times*, Technology Section, November 3, 2000.

to foreign nationals within the United States. Former Soviet IT specialists have found lucrative employment with such outsourcing companies. The reality of the New Economy is that commercial life has gone global. Outsourcing is beneficial to many organizations with limited budgets, both public and private, that wish to gain efficiencies and economies or to benefit from best practices. One key challenge in the realm of outsourcing is the current lack of due diligence and adequate risk assessment when partners are selected. Most subcontracts, and even their subcontractors, are not monitored closely, and insufficient attention is paid to potential problems.

At the heart of the information security conundrum is the prevalence of behavioral problems endemic to the Information Age: even where good security procedures are in place in government and private organizations, they often are ignored or violated because they are too complex or cumbersome. Government staff and company employees operate under extreme time pressures, and their top priority is to meet their responsibilities—possibly at the expense of security. For example, they might do classified work on a laptop while at home or traveling. The challenge of ensuring proper remote handling of sensitive or classified data will be compounded by a recent government initiative to encourage telecommuting.[12] The issues of security and accountability (e.g., for lost or compromised data) have not been thought through by the agencies monitoring the trend toward work outside the office. There are policies in place, but rarely are systemic audits carried out and enforced.

A recent example of damage caused by sheer human neglect is the case of Western Union, where a worker performing system maintenance inadvertently left open the firewall—a barrier of hardware or software to protect a Web site from unauthorized access. As a result,15,700 accounts were compromised, and the damage to Western Union's formerly solid reputation in the marketplace was considerable. Many recent instances of stolen credit card numbers or compromised personal data are due to the inadequate use of firewalls or to the lack of personal precautions with "always-on" home connections via digital subscriber line (DSL). These technologies and remedies are simple and cost-effective. The central problem is a lack of education and awareness. For the average consumer, ease of use currently takes precedence over security, and software therefore typically is designed with only those security features that will not be cumbersome to the consumer. Thus, sophisticated encryption and multiple layers of firewalls are shunned for speed, accessibility of data, and minimal password memorization. As incidents of cyber disruption, crime, and manipulation increase in both numbers and visibility, and stated vulnerabilities are proven, the tradeoffs between improving protection and preserving efficiency will undoubtedly be reevaluated, on both a corporate and a societal level.

---

12. The initiative was sponsored by President Clinton's secretary of transportation, Rodney Slater, who asked cabinet secretaries and agency heads to have 20 percent of their eligible employees in the Washington, D.C., area telecommuting by the year 2005. This represents roughly 70,000 federal workers telecommuting on any given day. For details, see Colleen O'Hara, "Government Raises Bar on Telework," *Federal Computer Week*, October 25, 2000.

# CHAPTER 3

# Putting Cyber Threats in a Global Context

## The Illusion of National Borders

With information technologies becoming increasingly small, cheap, fast, and ubiquitous, national infrastructures and critical domestic assets are undergoing rapid and inevitable internationalization. The growing codependence of public and private organizations on common systems, networks, and COTS hardware and software is shifting the ownership of these infrastructures and assets into the hands of those with the most efficient research, development, and production. While the private sector progresses rapidly and independently with new software development, and often with international corporate collaboration, the bureaucratic procedures embedded in the public sectors of most national governments prevent them from keeping pace. As groups working across regions and borders clamor for shrink-wrapped, standardized products, the lack of "biological diversity" in existing software packages and the emergence of open source software create profound security loopholes. International collaboration and outsourcing of research and management, software development, and coding for common operating systems compound the difficulty for private and, especially, public entities to place boundaries on their systems and networks.

National borders are not lines that can be transposed onto the map of information infrastructure, because ownership of and responsibility for the network becomes increasingly diverse as the level of detail increases. On a general level, the major pieces of the infrastructure can be said to be owned by a few large telecommunications providers in the private sector or as entities in partially socialized economies. With this definition, one might argue that where the physical cable is owned by the United States or its citizens, the boundaries can be drawn. Unfortunately, however, the information infrastructure of interest to the United States does not necessarily coincide with the major trunks and relay points in the network, because U.S. interests can exist as nodes within wholly foreign-owned network infrastructure. To effectively develop a doctrine for dealing with national information infrastructure protection, the definition of what is a national asset must be adjusted to reflect this reality.

# A Global Perspective

Incidents that were once locally confined now can have international repercussions and cross both public and private lines. Actual information warfare (IW) and cyberwar are still difficult to carry out on a large scale. IW strategies, however, are increasingly becoming embedded in national defense plans and intelligence operations, not only in the United States, but also in countries like the United Kingdom, France, Israel, China, and Russia. Although many experts believe that the threat from nation-states is currently overstated, the potential for sophisticated cyberwar tactics is likely to evolve rapidly.[13] In addition, gathering intelligence on information attacks poses strong challenges legally and operationally. Although no serious nation-based attacks have been detected to date, it is noteworthy that many documented attacks have had national organizations behind them or have supported nationalist motives: for example, persistent probes of U.S. businesses, universities, and government agencies by Russians; economic espionage by French companies and French intelligence; and attacks by Palestinian or pro-Palestinian groups on the Web sites of U.S. companies that actively do business with Israel.

In contrast to the still nebulous threat from nation-states, the threat from sub-groups and terrorist organizations is very real. While their goal is neither war nor destruction on a large scale, the effects of attacks from politically motivated groups are likely to be more widespread, if not as destructive as the effects of a state-sponsored attack. Their goals can be disruption, intimidation, or publication of a political message, as many previously discussed examples illustrate. Accuracy and scale are less important to nationally motivated hackers than general disruption. Few cyber incidents to date have qualified as "terrorist" as measured in the conventional sense. Most incidents have been criminal ones (theft of information, data, and code), or acts of cyber thrill-seeking, denial-of-service, and virus release. While loss of life is not a concern with these sorts of attacks, the damage has generally been quantifiable in dollar amounts that command respect and deserve attention. The cost of lost information, interrupted operations, damage to documents, server cleanups, overtime for IT employees, and the like quickly adds up. For example, losses from the Love Bug worm alone have been estimated as high as $8 billion.[14] The disruptive Melissa virus, although not damaging to files and systems, nonetheless caused many companies to shut down their e-mail systems to disinfect them. The business and financial losses caused by that downtime are impossible to measure, but clearly significant.

On the "hacktivist" front, the internationalization of the Internet has made it an important medium for coalescing disparate groups into common action—on a permanent or temporary basis—around one or more issues, with profound international repercussions. The impact of the disruptions at the 1999 World Trade

---

13. Of note, it is very difficult to assess the precise risk of any form of information attack. The experts who believe that the risk is "overstated" sometimes are thinking in terms of traditional threat assessment models, which look for big footprints, and may not be appropriate to the much more subtle and obscure cyber threats.

14. A large proportion of these losses were indirect, due to companies shutting down their servers as a protective measure.

Organization (WTO) Ministerial Conference in Seattle, spurred by interest groups and nongovernmental organizations uniting online, is once again not quantifiable in conventional terms, but is significant. The activists overcame national and international objectives to push their anticapitalist global agenda. Subsequently, although with lesser effects, they rallied to disrupt meetings in Washington, D.C., and World Bank and International Monetary Fund (IMF) meetings in Prague. The momentum achieved in assailing the negotiations in Seattle arguably could not have been achieved without the enabling medium of the Internet. Many have credited the Internet with the resonant political success of other grassroots movements such as the campaign that led to the international Treaty to Ban Landmines.

National governments, and specifically the U.S. government, have been slow to react to cyber vulnerabilities, even when faced with the evidence. There are many reasons for this. On the personnel side, there is a shortage of technical experts, a lack of adequate training for nontechnical employees using information systems to handle sensitive information, and insufficient employee background checks to hedge against insider threats. The intelligence community, while enforcing stricter information management rules due to the classified nature of much of its data, finds itself with similar limitations with respect to technically skilled analysts. Moreover, the community is extremely fragmented organizationally and is risk averse when it comes to addressing cyber issues. Law enforcement agencies are underfunded and understaffed and have shown themselves to be limited in their information sharing and dissemination due to the importance of their own information protection mission. Their focus on successful prosecution comes at the expense of a much-needed emphasis on prevention. Pervasive social concerns about privacy have also preoccupied government at a time when private information is more exposed than it ever has been, and the balance between privacy and public safety—which are complementary, not mutually exclusive—is constantly being renegotiated.

The availability of information enabled by the Internet has made both the infrastructure and its users subject to new levels of vulnerability. While the problems of infrastructure protection and cyber threats can be countered to some degree on a national level, a global perspective clearly is required for an effective overall response. As the most technologically advanced and powerful economy in the world, the United States has an obligation both domestically and internationally to provide leadership in ensuring that the increase in resources available to any given actor does not facilitate compromising the rights of individuals, corporations, and governments, or their respective assets.

# CHAPTER 4

# Net Assessment

## Where the Government and the Private Sector Stand

With such a broadly defined range of threats, it is hard to discuss in substantive terms what the role of the United States government and private-sector enterprises should be vis-à-vis cyber threats. The reality both domestically and internationally is, one, that the private sector owns most of the infrastructure but remains skeptical about the seriousness of the vulnerabilities and, two, that the government has done very little to make the case that larger threats to the infrastructure exist. Nonetheless, both government organizations and private corporations have taken steps to fulfill their obligations, and those capabilities should be looked at for their intentions, their results, and their potential effectiveness in addressing known and presumed threats.

## Government Assessment and Response

The United States government certainly has recognized the importance of national information infrastructure protection. Mandated activities within virtually every government agency have been put in place to target challenges to this mission, with varying degrees of effectiveness. Unfortunately, at a very basic level, the U.S. government has failed to define concretely what constitutes the national information infrastructure. In this context, providing an exhaustive list of government activities and policies to date is perhaps less useful than discussing, in a more general sense, what the government's obligations are and where the U.S. government has failed to fulfill them.

The U.S. government has an obligation to protect citizens and their assets from foreign and domestic threats of all kinds. In the case of cyber threats, a definition of national information infrastructure assets is a crucial starting point. The government's obligation should include all aspects, physical and informational, of defending and ensuring the functional reliability of any non-nodal segment of the global network. It should encompass, to varying degrees, the defense of networks and systems that are necessary for the continuation of government, for the continuing efficacy of U.S. armed forces, for the continued growth and stability of the economy, and for the safety of the public. In all of these cases, this responsibility applies to threats both foreign and domestic, from any level of actor ranging from individual up to nation-state, and whether criminal, political, or military in intent.

Government also must stipulate clear provisions for countering or punishing attacks. This obligation includes basic definitions of which acts—using U.S. infrastructure—are legal and which are not; which types of activities reasonably warrant a law enforcement response; and which types of activities qualify as acts of war against the national interest.

By almost any standard, the U.S. government has yet to meet the obligations delineated above. It also has failed to provide law enforcement, military, and intelligence capabilities commensurate with the challenge, as well as the necessary investments in research and defensive and offensive tools to fulfill national security objectives. A clear delegation of authority or chain of command both in the prevention and remediation of cyber attacks is still lacking. There also is no clear-cut authority for dealing with the issue of national information infrastructure protection. Even though certain agencies such as Space Command and the National Infrastructure Protection Center (NIPC) have been assigned general duties, the parameters of their responsibilities are nebulous at best and leave clear gaps in the defense of national assets.

Compounding the problem, the intelligence community lacks the funding and analytical sophistication to effectively pursue Internet activities. Insufficient leadership has hindered innovative or effective work and limited growth in technical and analytic capabilities. The law enforcement community also has so far failed to effectively adapt its investigative tactics to Information Age indicators and methodologies, and its very mission prevents it from effectively engaging in either warning or information sharing, both crucial facets of prevention.[15] Lastly, efforts by DOD to monitor its networks are fraught with interservice rivalries and a basic lack of technical capability to oversee a widely dispersed set of assets. DOD does house excellent efforts such as SHADOW at the Naval Surface Warfare Center-Dahlgren, which takes intrusion detection to a new level of performance by stepping away from a focus on predefined attacks and instead using artificial intelligence to look for and identify unusual activity. This is precisely the kind of effort required to develop the capabilities to protect national infrastructure assets in the long term. In addition, a much greater degree of transparency between law enforcement and national security organizations in intrusion detection, response, investigation, and prosecution also is necessary, as the responses differ and cyber timelines are measured not in days or hours, but in minutes and seconds.

While none of these problems is insoluble, they do reflect a systemic problem—a lack of leadership. Even without looking at broader infrastructural concerns, the heads of government organizations have paid insufficient attention to their internal information technology security problems. The challenge is less one of funding than one of behavior, processes, policy, decisionmaking, follow-through, and cross-agency communication. To be effective in meeting its obligations to its citizens, the U.S. government must begin by initiating better security practices within its own organizations and addressing information security issues at a level far beyond the current (often rhetorical) measures.

---

15. The weaknesses of the NIPC model in particular are discussed in chapter 5, "New Processes."

# Private-Sector Assessment and Response

Because so much of the critical value and ownership of the infrastructure is in private hands, the private sector plays a significant and often uncomfortable role in information infrastructure protection. Businesses, institutions, and corporations all increasingly depend on the Internet for both commercial and personal transactions. The security of the information infrastructure therefore is becoming as critical to their success, solvency, and continuity of operations as the protection of telephone, power, or transportation systems. Many companies recognized their dependencies early on, as well as their need for appropriate security measures (both technical and behavioral). These corporations—in particular financial institutions, utilities groups, and software companies—not only have undertaken internal precautionary measures; many are starting to publicly convey a message of increased protection. Until recently, security was not included in marketplace pitches for new software and tools. But security is now a growing part of the corporate message.

By contrast, other, often smaller companies appear blissfully unaware of the threat or choose not to expend the personnel and resources necessary to protect themselves. Corporate cultures often are slow to react to threats until a clear example of the costs of failing to exercise due care drives the point home.

The private sector's obligation with respect to protecting the national information infrastructure is uniquely different from other infrastructure-related national security concerns. Because the U.S. government cannot realistically monitor the entire infrastructure, private entities from individuals to major multinational corporations must provide for their own basic defense. Beyond a reasonable level, this responsibility converts over to government hands. In practical terms, this line of obligation is akin to the private responsibility of locking up one's home to prevent theft. It is conceptually harder, though, for organizations and individuals to grasp the value of less tangible assets such as information and access. Therefore, security measures taken in the virtual world do not parallel those taken for granted in the physical world.

Underestimating the costs of a failure in information infrastructure is probably the deciding factor in ensuring the low level of interest in the subject by the private sector. This is due to some extent to the difficulty of estimating the cost of damages, and the widely varying estimates used in the media do little to lend weight to the potential threat. Commercial organizations, as well as government agencies, are still learning to take advantage of the opportunities present in a networked environment. As such, they have not yet reacted effectively to use the capabilities available to protect themselves, nor have they recognized the business-case importance of doing their part to protect information infrastructure.

The problem is certainly not one of resources. On the technical side, the private sector in the United States has ample access to cheap, efficient, and high-quality security products with low implementation and maintenance costs. On the behavioral side, commercial organizations frequently form industry associations and trade groups to represent their collective interests in spite of their individually competitive nature. Effective information sharing is one of the most critical aspects to effective information infrastructure protection and could be an area in which the private sector truly excels. But no particular industry or trade either owns or is disproportionately dependent on the information infrastructure, leaving a leadership void in the cause of spreading awareness of problems, threats, and solutions. Commercial organizations generally rely on government to provide the means of communication when the distribution channels are diverse and scattered.

Because it has access to data identifying vulnerabilities and ongoing threats, the government is in a unique position—and has a unique obligation—to provide the public with the motivation it needs to undertake the protective measures that the marketplace has neglected. Unfortunately, when addressing private entities, the government generally has stressed national security arguments rather than making its case on more tangible economic factors. In the coming years, it will be essential for the U.S. government to modify its rhetoric and engage in a real dialogue with those who control and own significant parts of the information infrastructure. Concurrently, it must build on positive measures already in existence in the private sector and take on a much more prominent leadership role in educating the public on infrastructure questions, vulnerabilities, and solutions.

# CHAPTER 5

# New Processes

## Toward Viable Cyber Policies and Public-Private Relationships

### An Increased Public-Private Dialogue and Improved Public-Private Partnerships

Improved and enhanced mechanisms for information sharing will be the crucial first step in any government initiative to convince the private sector that it needs to do more to hedge against cyber threats. Information sharing must be part of a larger government strategy, wherein communication takes place not only between government and the private sector but between different government agencies, particularly between the national security and law enforcement communities. "Information sharing" is a broad and complex concept; however, certain forms of information are more crucial in improving the prevention of cyber incidents and also are more readily shared among groups and institutions. The critical types of information that government and industry should exchange are the following:

- *Known network vulnerabilities.* If a company or government agency has carried out an assessment of its own networks and generated data, it can act to secure its systems more effectively and can share the nature of some of its former vulnerabilities with others, to save them both time and risk. A barrier to this type of sharing emerges when there are legal concerns over due diligence. For instance, if a company or agency remedies only 90 percent of identified vulnerabilities in its own systems—and benefits others by sharing that information— does that constitute a punishable violation of the standard of care? One of the problems experienced by the NIPC, by virtue of its location within the Federal Bureau of Investigation (FBI), is that those in charge of information sharing are first and foremost prosecutors and law enforcement officers.

- *Warning of ongoing attacks or threats,* without "sources and methods" attribution. The individuals likely to first detect intrusions or attacks are system administrators and network administrators. But they are reluctant to report these intrusions to law enforcement, as they fear that proprietary information will be compromised or that their corporate reputation will suffer if the intrusions are made public. When ongoing attacks are reported, law enforcement should find ways of sanitizing the information, analyzing it, and disseminating it among the organizations that also could be affected, thus identifying potential vulnerabilities or attacks without naming the institution or company under attack. This information sharing by law enforcement is particularly crucial in the case of systematic attacks or probes that are known to law enforcement because they are pervasive enough to be a national security concern or because they originate in a specific foreign nation. Law enforcement has a poor track record of sharing such information with the private sector. The CERT at Carnegie Mellon, however, has provided early warning information to system administrators in a relatively efficient manner and generally receives positive feedback from private-sector entities.

- *Strategies for defending against certain types of attack.* When an individual institution locates a vulnerability, or is made aware of one, and finds a solution, it resists sharing that information because of the proprietary value of its solution. Again, the government function should be to sanitize and disseminate the information in a way that supports prevention for other companies but does not reveal the identity of the company providing the solution. Companies could be asked to provide information on new viruses, the apparent modus operandi of a given attacker (what the hacker has taken or damaged, what he/she appears to be looking for), or information gleaned from meetings with hackers who have identified specific targets for attack. This will help establish and identify signatures and improve sensors for better protection in the future.

Because of recent negative trends in information sharing, and to provide an added incentive to the private sector, government must show that it is willing to initiate the dialogue, to "share first." Effective cooperation will flow from capitalizing on comparative advantages. The government has the core insights on critical infrastructure protection from a national security perspective (although the power companies, telecommunications providers, and financial institutions have effective backup systems and contingency plans in place to hedge against normal outages, natural disasters, and the like). The private sector, on the other hand, has the core insights on information security management.

Aside from the organizations set up as a result of Presidential Decision Directive (PDD) 63,[16] another recent—and very successful—model for public-private information sharing is the clearinghouse set up for Y2K. Information from the national Y2K database was shared and accessed across public, private, and even international lines. The rules for access were clear and binding. Companies were asked to sign nondisclosure agreements before they could access information on existing vulnerabilities, and a large number of companies signed up. Both the president's National Security Telecommunications Advisory Committee (NSTAC) and the National Coordinating Center for Telecommunications (NCC) have already taken steps toward applying this model to current initiatives. Industry also frequently has used the NCC as a go-between for sharing information between private corporations.

---

16. PDD 63 was promulgated in May 1998 and established a structure to protect critical infrastructure. Among other things, PDD 63 created a National Coordinator for Security, Counter-Terrorism and Infrastructure Protection; a National Infrastructure Protection Center (NIPC); a National Infrastructure Assurance Council (NIAC); and a Critical Infrastructure Assurance Office (CIAO).

Due to the positive Y2K precedent, they trust the NCC with information sanitation and protection.

In the wake of recent viruses and more serious hacking incidents, the government has successfully established its role as a facilitator in meetings between leaders in specific industries that have a stake in information security. For example, a recent White House conference brought together business-to-business (B2B) companies to discuss software security. The government was the catalyst for a gathering that would not have taken place on its own. Even if information sharing develops slowly, the government facilitation of fora for discussion and face-to-face meetings will help build relationships between government entities and industry leaders and between individual companies within a given industry. These relationships in and of themselves will be of significant value, as they will foster more active cooperation during an operational emergency, be it due to a natural disaster or to an actual attack. On an equally positive note, private-sector attendance at the Partnership for Critical Infrastructure Security meetings has grown steadily to include several hundred companies. While this number is still a small percentage of the aggregate, the increased participation is indicative of a positive trend toward more comprehensive gatherings. In addition, experience has shown that companies that are not always willing to listen to government nonetheless will listen to each other, so increased participation has positive ripple effects.

Following the recommendations of PDD 63, associations are already forming within business sectors to share information, and many lead sectors have begun a dialogue with lead government agencies. These information sharing and analysis centers (ISACs) are a strong positive model of successful cooperation and initiative. Although the centers function within industry, most of them have a direct mechanism for communicating with the government and sharing information not only among their membership, but across private-public lines. Active ISACs include the following:

■ THE BANKING AND FINANCE ISAC. Although members of this sector are making progress, they are reluctant to share information with the government (and sometimes with each other) due to anonymity concerns, protection under the Freedom of Information Act, discovery rules, and fear of regulation stemming from familiarity. Nonetheless, they were able to warn companies and government agencies about the Love Bug virus eight hours before the National Infrastructure Protection Center (NIPC) did.

■ THE TELECOMMUNICATIONS ISAC. This sector had previously formed alliances under Department of Defense leadership and officially established an ISAC in March 2000. While the telecommunications industry also is selective about sharing information with government, it has shown more willingness to be open than its counterparts in other industries. The NSTAC, which is the industry advisory body to the president, shares information as a byproduct of its advisory function. It is effective, but also has the support of full-time government staff and a government agency acting as secretariat. This model might be difficult to replicate for industries with larger numbers of representatives, but should nonetheless be considered.

■ THE NORTH AMERICAN ELECTRIC RELIABILITY COUNCIL (NERC) ISAC. The electric power industry is working with the NERC to report cyber outages as well as hard power outages and is sharing this information with the NIPC. The NERC ISAC currently enjoys a greater membership than any other ISAC and has generated roughly 75 reports that have formed the basis for analysis and warning bulletins shared among the members.

■ THE INFORMATION TECHNOLOGY ISAC. A group of companies has now committed to contribute to the IT sector ISAC, with 19 companies committing to serve as founding members. This ISAC is of particular importance as it brings together representatives from different parts of the IT world, many of whom handle and address very different pieces of complex IT systems and networks. These parts, while different, are inherently complementary. Increased communication within this sector and, potentially, between sectors and with government signifies a substantial initial step in information sharing on cyber threats, infrastructure vulnerabilities, and timely, proactive solutions.

Other industries are establishing relatively successful cooperative mechanisms outside of the ISAC model. One example is the Information Technology Association of America (ITAA), which has brought together members of the IT industry to begin moving toward increased cooperation. The IT sector faces greater challenges than the more interconnected utilities, because, as has been noted, every company produces or sells pieces of the sector, and there is little overlap or homogeneity.

The NIPC—housed within the Department of Justice and initially touted as one of the most promising models proposed in PDD 63—has largely failed in its information coordination duties due to lack of trust, lack of reciprocal sharing, and lack of guarantees or incentives. The private sector often has expressed concern that it has shared information with the NIPC but has gotten no information in return. There also have been examples in which law enforcement was made aware of ongoing attacks, but did not inform the companies under attack for several weeks, even months, in order that the FBI might carry out its research.[17] That said, the NIPC initiative is a good start that must be supplemented with more robust models such as those listed above.[18] Moreover, it should be noted that the NIPC's InfraGard program—which endeavors to provide an information-sharing mechanism for

---

17. For examples of the NIPC's shortcomings, corroborated by experts in both government and the private sector, see Lewis Z. Koch, "Cybercriminals on the Loose," *ZDNet: Interactive Week,* November 6, 2000.

18. Certain measures proposed or adopted by Congress have been either too ambitious or too short-sighted and fail to address the crux of the problem. For example, the Internet Integrity and Critical Infrastructure Act of 2000 (S. 2448) elevates the top job at the Justice Department's Computer Crime and Intellectual Property section to the level of deputy assistant attorney general, but does not address the thorny issue of Internet surveillance. The act also makes the Secret Service responsible for the investigation and prosecution of cyber attacks on financial institutions, an area that the FBI has not yet been willing to cede. Several important provisions were removed from the original bill, including those related to spam, international computer crime enforcement, identity theft, and satellite subscriber privacy. The bill also includes a controversial forfeitures provision, which would make companies the targets of forfeitures if insiders hack into their systems while on the job.

intrusion incidents and vulnerability assessments on a local level—has spawned some highly successful local chapters; these work with FBI field offices and have been particularly effective at providing education and training for local businesses and industries.

In evaluating progress to date, it is important to note that the Freedom of Information Act has been a significant obstacle to public-private information sharing, because companies (1) run the risk of having sensitive or proprietary data compromised if it is revealed to the public, and (2) fear damage to shareholder confidence if vulnerabilities are publicly acknowledged. The recent example of the hack into Microsoft Corporation, cited previously, illustrates this fear of sharing information with law enforcement. It is worth exploring whether FOIA exceptions can be made to enhance the role of the ISACs and of the other existing and proposed information-sharing mechanisms discussed above. A solid initiative was proposed in October 2000 by Senators Jon Kyl (R-Ariz.) and Dianne Feinstein (D-Calif.), in the form of the Cyber Security Enhancement Act of 2000 (S. 3188). According to Senator Kyl, this bill "would allow companies to voluntarily submit information on cyber vulnerabilities, threats, and attacks to the federal government, without this information being subject to FOIA disclosure. . . . This legislation would only protect voluntarily submitted information that the government would otherwise not have."[19]

To build on previous efforts and ensure the effectiveness of information-sharing mechanisms across the spectrum, a single point of national coordination for reporting and responding to cyber threats should be established. This point of contact would be a cyber security "commander" (or "national CIO"), at the helm of a "virtual" crisis management center that would include a confidential cyber-911 function, with distributed regional offices and call centers. The central point of contact would provide "THREATCON" alerts similar to the DEFCON levels (DEFense CONditions for nuclear forces) and INFOCON levels (suggested, but not yet implemented, for information attacks) employed by the Department of Defense. The virtual center would act as a warning center that, in the case of a virus or denial-of-service attack, would instantly disseminate relevant, sanitized information and attempt to have the warning spread faster than the attack itself. The center also would act as a public relations channel for many of the public-private communications described above. The 911 function will be most effective if it is combined with the implementation of a cyber-411 function, in other words, a multi-tiered "yellow pages" catering to all strata of information security consumers, from mom-and-pop shops to state- and national-level government organizations to multinational private corporations. The center could work in conjunction with the Critical Infrastructure Assurance Office (CIAO), housed in the Department of Commerce, which has been positively viewed by private-sector groups for its efforts at cooperation with the private sector to fulfill its public education mission.

So as not to repeat negative experiences, it is important that this center of coordination lie outside of the Department of Justice. Experience has shown that the

---

19. In his October testimony, Senator Kyl also noted that more than 100 exceptions to the FOIA have been created by other laws to date.

Department of Justice has not been a good home for the NIPC for reasons described above. When the FBI is in charge of coordinating information sharing, and yet must protect information because of its law enforcement mission, the mechanisms for reciprocity and trust break down. The FBI's operations are focused on and reward successful prosecution. The incentive structures for prevention currently built into its mission are grossly insufficient. Arguably, the new virtual center described above should replace the NIPC in order to reestablish relationships of trust and reciprocity.

A task force should be set up by the Bush administration to determine the best location for such a center, be it in the White House, the Department of Defense, or the Department of Commerce, or managed as a shared entity among multiple organizations. A successful multiagency model already exists in the form of the National Communication System (NCS), established in the 1960s after the Bay of Pigs fiasco to coordinate communications and national command authorities in emergencies (military or natural disaster). Although DOD is its executive agent, the NCS takes its policy direction from the Office of Science and Technology Policy (OSTP), the National Security Council (NSC), and the Office of Management and Budget (OMB). The NCS has a proven mechanism in place to coordinate dialogue among 23 departments and agencies, as well as with the private sector, to plan and respond in an emergency. It thus might serve either as an ideal locus or as an ideal model for the new virtual center.

In general, relationships between the public and private sectors must be voluntary, goal-oriented, and focused on managed expectations, mutual trust, and frequent and lasting interaction. Speaking the same language and understanding each other's priorities will be critical to this exchange. As noted previously, the government often has presented the issue of cyber threats to the private sector in national security language, when a dialogue would be better fostered if the urgency of the matter were expressed in terms of business losses and impact on consumer confidence. New, innovative companies lack the institutional knowledge to work with the government to protect shared networks, while motivations of consumers (which drive profits) are speed, ease of use, and features—not security. At the same time, surveys show that security and privacy are increasingly important to e-commerce customers, a finding that has motivated many companies to take greater security precautions. Government sensitivity to the evolving nature of consumer demands and business priorities will provide the appropriate "cultural" background to facilitate improved communications.

## Government Actions to Motivate and Remove Barriers to Private-Sector Actions

The central challenge in providing incentives is quantifying the risk and evaluating risk-sharing and risk-management models. Risk in cyber attacks is difficult to quantify because of the lack of experience and actuarially based data. As deaths currently are unlikely to result from hacking, the end-state is not likely to be as dramatic as it has been in other industries that have galvanized insurance and litigation processes (e.g., the automobile industry, where the need for seat belts or air bags is established based on clear statistics and dire end results). Government should be the catalyst for the establishment of parameters and standards, but not the enforcer. Industry should participate in establishing standards on a voluntary basis, based on its members' superior understanding of and investment in the various facets of information technology.

Some pragmatic suggestions of incentives that the government can provide to the private sector beyond information sharing include the following:

■ *Tax breaks or equivalent "credits"* can be established for companies that utilize certified safety products that have been inspected by an accredited organization and that also strictly enforce certain types of security procedures and behaviors. Similar credits can be provided to software companies such as Microsoft or Internet service providers such as America Online (AOL) to build improved security features into their commonly used packages—for example, more sophisticated encryption, firewall alerts, digital certificates, and so on.

■ The government should further *invest or co-invest in new technologies and in its own internal research and development* at agencies such as the Defense Advanced Research Projects Agency (DARPA). Public endorsement also should be provided clearly to companies that manufacture safety products or that expand their products' range—for example, the "digital immune system" concept for virus-scanning software recently developed by IBM and Symantec.

■ The government should facilitate a *private-sector dialogue and consensus-based mechanism for certifying the safety and effectiveness* of security products. Moody's Risk Management Services's "Quantitative Risk Analytics" tool might be effective in establishing a rating system for products and practices.

■ Insurance companies should be encouraged to include *limited liability indemnification insurance policies against cyber disruption* in their insurance portfolios. The American International Group, Inc. (AIG) and other insurance companies already are beginning to provide certain types of insurance against disruption (although of necessity, most products are very niche-oriented, have associated restrictions, and are emerging in incremental stages). Many of these companies have been working with the CIAO to assess how best to respond to threats to business operations, and they should be given public recognition for their efforts. Companies such as AIG assess the risk as liability, compromised or lost information, and interruption of service, but also as less tangible potential damage in the form of tarnished reputations or loss of trade secrets. Thus, classic business insurance that protects tangible assets cannot apply in the cyber realm. AIG recommends liability coverage that will address four elements: privacy; disclosure of customer information; transmission of a virus ("downstream liability"); and denial of service lawsuits.[20]

---

20. AIG also provides protection against Web content or media liabilities; loss of property (information assets); loss of e-business during denial-of-service or other crippling attacks; and cyber extortion (as happened recently to the company CD Universe). AIG suggests providing instant awards leading to hacker arrests and acquiring crisis communication management coverage.

- Insurance companies should join forces with security technology companies to *establish basic requirements for coverage,* and government can once again provide the role of facilitator. Insurers could require that minimum standards be met, and might underwrite the establishment of organizations to set those standards. The top information security firms already have checklists for companies to use in evaluating their security practices. These could be used as the basis for evaluation by insurance companies.

- *Liability limits against disruption of service* can be established if a company utilizes certified products and meets established "best practices." These practices would be evaluated based on annual (or biannual) inspections. The inspections are critical, as certified components are not sufficient in and of themselves for prevention. The design of the overall system, the implementation and configuration of the design, the maintenance and upkeep of the configuration, and the provision of measures for physical security and personnel security are all necessary as well.[21] In addition, careful consideration should be given to a proposal to grant relief from antitrust laws to like-minded corporations that share information and collaborate purely in matters of information security.

- *Clear corporate liability* should be established to transfer risk from the shoulders of consumers onto the companies providing software or services. Most companies have become very dependent on the Internet, and many are wide open to significant liabilities they are not paying much attention to. This risk transfer would encourage companies both to purchase insurance and to improve their fraud detection or intrusion detection systems. This process has proven highly successful with the credit card industry, where the passing of the Electronic Fund Transfer Act imposed limitations on the amount of consumer liability ($50 if the financial institution was notified by the consumer within two business days, and $500 if the consumer did not provide timely notice).

- *Personal liability and accountability* should be encouraged not only within government but also for the CIOs, CEOs, and boards of directors that govern private corporations. Establishing clear lines of responsibility will encourage more stringent security measures and practices within companies. The Institute of Internal Auditors has begun addressing boards of directors and senior officers of corporations about their responsibilities in the arena of information systems protection and the potential for charges of criminal negligence to be

---

21. WarRoom Research (http://www.warroomresearch.com/security/securitysafeguards.htm) specifically notes the following areas of security critical to a "security life cycle" approach:

- **Technologies:** intrusion detection, firewalls, access control, encryption, identification and authentication, etc.
- **Processes:** business intelligence assessments, risk analysis, vulnerability assessments, security architecture development and evaluation, implementation plans, security tests and evaluation, etc.
- **People:** security training and awareness, investigative support, continuity planning, warroom simulations, human resources guidance, etc.
- **Facilities:** data center operations, recovery services, data vaulting, enterprise information portals, etc.

brought if a certain level of vulnerability is demonstrated and fiduciary duties have been disregarded or violated. Of note, insurance companies already are offering directors-and-officers' (DNO) insurance to permit corporate leaders to protect themselves from shareholder actions. In the case of privacy rules, some institutions and corporations recently have begun passing on the responsibility for the protection of private and sensitive information to the individual employees who handle it, providing a further incentive for increased personnel sensitivity to best practices.

- *Extraordinary liability relief* should be provided in the case of cyberwarfare, similar to indemnification authorities for destruction of commercial assets through conventional warfare. In addition, financial relief for digital "disasters" akin to natural disasters (flood relief, earthquake relief) should be given careful consideration. In the latter case, insurance executives have suggested that the government should be the "insurer of last resort." Insurance companies would insure up to a certain level (still to be determined); a consortium of insurance, software, and hardware companies could create a pool for reinsurance purposes; and the government would intervene in cases of massive outages or shutdowns.

- *Intermediate regulatory steps* should be suggested for systems that are common to public and private entities. There are several precedents for the domestic and international regulation of shared systems, for example, in air and sea transport policies, or in the control of infectious diseases. As with the issue of mandates, the problem of quantifying risk is important—infectious diseases lead to significant casualties, while cyber incidents have not (yet). The budding international collaboration on encryption and privacy issues might also be used as a point of reference in a G-8 or other international approach to the issue of system regulation.

# CHAPTER 6

# Actionable Institutional Fixes
Initiatives to Address Problems within
Government

## Government Leadership by Example

The government will be effective in its efforts to motivate the private sector only if it improves its own processes, behaviors, systems, and communications. While certain agencies and departments such as the National Security Council, the Department of Defense, and the Department of Commerce have already devoted considerable strategic thinking to the problem, the need for improved implementation is strong.

The most crippling aspect of the U.S. government's failures in addressing the issue of information infrastructure protection is the lack of a clear government statement defining the problem, the locus of authority and responsibility for defense, and the chain of command in the event of an attack. As stated earlier, the government has yet to articulate a commonly agreed-upon, clearly defined position on what it considers an information attack and on how and under what conditions it will respond. Without this fundamental policy premise, it is very difficult—if not impossible—to formulate event sequence scenarios that would involve planning, defense, and response. This in turn complicates the task of devising viable forms of timely and effective reaction or retaliation, as well as realistic offensive information warfare (IW) and information operations (IO) capabilities. National information infrastructure protection must be viewed as an ongoing concern, rather than as a series of disjointed incidents of varying magnitudes.

One of the challenges the government faces in providing motivation to the private sector is not only its poor articulation of the problem, but also its weak track record of leadership by example. To wit, the government recently received a D-minus grade in a congressional review of systems security. The problems are less technological than they are behavioral. An ideal starting point is more effective protection of government systems, including simple measures such as installing virus-protection software upgrades and patches in a timely manner. In addition to demonstrating competence by establishing more effective protection of its own systems, government can provide incentives such as procurement and grant programs to encourage the same level of information systems and network protection in academia and in state and local governments, and it can implement measures discussed in the previous chapter.

As a reaction to the D-minus grade, the Department of Defense already has undertaken specific measures to bolster its systems security. In particular, the Pentagon announced in November 2000 that it was incorporating the use of biometrics into its systems and adopting specific measures to better manage the use and restriction of mobile code (software that moves over a network in the interaction between a Web browser and a server). DOD also is seeking to enhance information sharing across agencies by working on the completion of a common database that would enable CERTs across DOD, intelligence agencies, and the FBI to share information critical to protecting their networks against intruders. In response to a March 2000 annual survey by the FBI and the Computer Security Institute, which revealed that 70 percent of large government organizations had detected serious computer-security breaches in the previous 12 months, national laboratories such as Sandia have begun running "red team" exercises as an integral part of testing and evaluating their security systems design.[22]

## Moving Away from the Passive Response Posture

Without a clear statement of the problem or a viable strategic policy premise in place, all critical agencies within the United States government currently default to a passive response posture against all aggressors—be they foreign governments, commercial interests, hacktivists, or criminals. This posture compounds existing challenges and creates further dangers for many reasons. Nations and nonstate actors that do not operate under "Western values" see a passive posture as a sign of weakness that creates targets of opportunity. The risk calculus applied by terrorist elements to conventional forms of terrorism or to attacks involving weapons of mass destruction applies in the case of information attacks as well. An aggressor who is willing to take serious risks and use violence as a policy position will be encouraged by the perception of a passive response posture. A doctrine of passive response also undermines efforts geared at identifying attackers and deterring future hostile acts.

In addition, as discussed earlier, expansion in the global use of information weapons for troublemaking, political, or criminal purposes has created a significant noise floor of spurious incidents that can shroud serious hostile activities, which may include espionage, intelligence collection, and state-sponsored network mapping or information attacks. This haze—referred to in more conventional terms as the "fog of war"—makes it increasingly difficult for the government to discern between legitimate threats to national security and the acts of common criminals or thrill-seeking hackers.

Still, although rapid identification of perpetrators remains a challenge, the technical capabilities for remediation, tactical response, and investigation (trap-and-trace) increase in sophistication daily. Fog-of-war problems can be addressed on a technical level by investing real resources into tracking the flow of information

---

22. For more detail on Sandia's red team projects, see W. Wayt Gibbs, "Red Team versus the Agents," *Scientific American,* December 2000.

through packet-switching routing networks like the Internet. The obstacles to an effective response to information attacks remain primarily in the realms of policy, mindset, and personnel, particularly in law enforcement and intelligence. For example, DOD's priority within a passive response posture is to thwart attacks, not to identify or retaliate against perpetrators. When no response is intended, the incentive structure for identifying perpetrators breaks down.

The United States should not find itself in such a position. The U.S. government must deliberately move to an active response posture, providing the necessary incentives and legal premises for agencies to act quickly and intelligently to defend the national assets that fall within their purview. The response against information attacks must be part of a broad and clearly articulated national response plan, ensuring the capability to respond immediately to an attack or to counter a known threat, irrespective of its origin—domestic, international, state-sponsored, or subnational. Additionally, a serious analytic cadre should be built and maintained to support investigations and activities on an ongoing basis.

## Responding at the Speed of Business

A critical element of adopting a comprehensive, active response policy is to greatly increase the speed of response to cyber incidents, particularly those with potentially cascading effects throughout the infrastructure. In spite of the response problem clearly identified in comprehensive governmentwide and infrastructurewide exercises such as Eligible Receiver, government responses to real (subsequent) incidents such as Solar Sunrise and Moonlight Maze have been thoroughly inadequate.[23] While modest efforts were made to increase interagency cooperation and to learn from failed attempts at real-time responses, timelines for responses have barely improved. Unlike "conventional" forms of warfare or terrorism, preparations for and the initiation of cyber attacks are not easily perceived. The anonymity of the Internet lends itself well to the covert and invisible launching of coordinated attacks, using the low-level noise mentioned previously as cover. Planning a three-month window to address hostile activities that may last for only seconds or min-

---

23. "Eligible Receiver" (ER97) was the code name for a "no notice" exercise run by the Pentagon in 1997, targeting government computer systems. Using COTS products and software available on the Internet, "red teams" composed of 25 to 35 government computer experts from the National Security Agency were able to penetrate a wide variety of computer systems in less than three months, including the Pentagon's Non-classified Internet Protocol Routing Network (NIPRNET). They also demonstrated the theoretical capability to shut down electrical power to major cities and to penetrate the classified Secret Internet Protocol Routing Network (SIPRNET). Red team penetrations were so extensive that the viability of the Global Command and Control System (GCCS) serving all unified commands was called into question. "Solar Sunrise" refers to the multiagency investigation into a series of attacks carried out by hackers between February and March 1998. More than 500 military, government, and private-sector computer systems were penetrated. Many initially thought the intrusions were linked to Iraq, because the United States was moving troops to the Persian Gulf region at that time and because some of the attacks were linked to Internet service providers in that region. The ensuing investigation determined that two youths from California and at least one individual in Israel were behind the system invasions.

utes, and for which varying degrees of immediate response must be available for both deterrence of further attacks and retribution against existing ones, is not a viable policy by any standard.

Many critical obstacles to improving the speed of response and the quality of both defense and retaliation are problems of internal policy and protocol. Improved interagency communication is as crucial as public-private information sharing mechanisms. The National Security Council and the executive branch must facilitate discussion and communication with and between law enforcement and intelligence and must provide a compelling case for organizations in these domains to focus on prevention as well as remediation. These functions will require the government-wide institution of norms for personal responsibility, accountability, and liability for violating or ignoring mandated security procedures, such as those described above for the private sector.

Concurrently, reward structures for assimilation of "best practices" into government institutions should balance out the threat of sanctions for noncompliance. Basic mechanisms for identifying and countering insider threats also are necessary, particularly in light of relaxed personal security requirements in many government areas over time (even while telling the private sector to make theirs more stringent). One example is the Single Scope Background Investigation (SSBI) required for security clearances. The investigations used to retain their validity for five years but now are applicable for seven years, even though the potential to violate the terms of these clearances has increased with the new technologies.

On a more ambitious level, and concurrently with the adoption of a more active response posture, the president should recommend measures similar to those suggested in previous PDDs to cover the issue of reconstitution and the need for contingency plans for cyber incidents. First-responder models are critical for the cyber world and arguably are more readily implementable (with sufficient technical staff) than those postulated for chemical or biological warfare and terrorism. As these issues have been studied extensively in the context of chemical, biological, radiological, and nuclear (CBRN) weapons, as well as in the discussions surrounding the mandate of the NIPC, costly studies and reports should not be necessary because previous data can readily be drawn upon. There also are well-established models through backup systems and degradation management systems for ensuring continuity of operations in the case of cyber attack. These models exist both within specific sectors (e.g., utilities) as a requirement for maintaining service during natural disasters and within plans developed in the late 1990s to address forecasted Y2K concerns.

## Educating Government Employees and the Public

At the core of solutions within the public sector is the need for vastly improved education and training. This includes promoting awareness of security issues as a central component of all government business; the encouragement of technical competency through continuing education and access to cutting-edge courses; personnel incentives for promotion and growth; a reevaluation of key retention factors such as competitive salaries and health care or other benefits; and a substantial increase in the number of cyber professionals through recruitment directly from undergraduate or graduate programs and through incentives to educational institutions.

Successful models already exist within specific sectors. For example, the National Cybercrime Training Partnership (NCTP) works across agencies (with DOJ chairmanship) to provide dynamic, multilevel, geographically decentralized training to federal, state, and local law enforcement agencies and officials on responding to electronic and high-technology crime. Another example is the "Cyber Corps" of computer experts, established by President Clinton, which received continued funding for fiscal year 2001. These efforts represent a good beginning, but they must be supplemented with mission-specific training for computer scientists and engineers hired into government service. This training must focus on building multiple competencies, to include a real military offensive network warfare capability, "cyber" counterintelligence analysts and operatives, human factors analysts who can ascertain motivations (to enable effective deterrent measures as well as an accurate damage assessment and appropriate response), and a competent public relations staff to effectively educate the public on the vulnerabilities of individual and networked PCs.

Education will be critical to promoting the supporting societal context for improvements in security-related behaviors in both private and public realms, and policies will need to be established to encourage the development of educational programs at all levels. The shortage of qualified information security experts not only points to the need to train security professionals on the job; it also highlights the need for improvement in computer science and MIS education, where security and systems reliability have not been important considerations in curriculum design. According to the Georgia Institute of Technology, in 1999 only ten U.S. citizens chose careers in computer security after completing a Ph.D. in computer science; in contrast, dozens of foreign students embraced the field. Currently, only ten tenured professors across all accredited U.S. universities specialize in information security.[24]

Government encouragement of and incentives for university funding for information security programs and faculty are essential. Recent initiatives have provided a positive step toward this goal. For example, in October 2000 then-President Clinton announced a "Scholarship for Service" program that will provide up to two years of scholarship funding for students studying information security in return for a commitment to work for an equal amount of time for the federal government. This initiative is one of five education and training programs stipulated under the federal National Plan for Information Systems Protection and will be administered

---

24. Source: Gene Spafford, Director of the Purdue Center for Education and Research in Information Assurance and Security (CERIAS), and founder of the Purdue Computer Emergency Response Team (PCERT).

by the National Science Foundation (NSF).[25] These measures are laudable, but not yet sufficient. Many experts argue the need to provide incentives for education long before the university years, for example, for information technology ethics courses at the primary school level.

## A Viable Legal Framework

Suggestions have been made throughout this report about legal steps—domestic as well as international—that would help to improve both defenses against cyber attacks and preventive measures for countering known cyber threats. A detailed discussion of domestic and international legislation governing prosecution issues is outside the scope of this report. There is, however, a pressing need for the following: legislation facilitating hack-back capabilities and trap-and-trace procedures; a clear legal definition for "cyber reconstitution"; the expansion of government capabilities to assist in the recovery of communications and information systems; and a collaborative dialogue with the private sector concerning antitrust and tort liability issues.[26]

It is also important to note the numerous legal constraints in the realm of international collaboration on addressing and countering cyber threats and prosecuting cyber attacks. Investigations and prosecutions of computer crime fly in the face of national sovereignty and give rise to jurisdictional issues. With roughly 210 countries on the Internet, individual sets of bilateral agreements would not be bureaucratically feasible. Therefore, common international platforms must be achieved.

The primary goals of any international agreement should be to achieve the following:

■ *Clearly define what constitutes a hostile act*, namely, where to draw the line between attack and annoyance (e.g., with denial-of-service attacks, defacement of Web pages, individual machines being compromised, and so on).

■ *Clearly define what actions are required for a legal response*, including whether a target must be notified before retribution is exacted and, if so, under what circumstances.

■ *Include language to facilitate working around technical problems and limitations*. In particular, this language should allow for a response policy that does not require certainty about the identity or even the nature of the source of the attack.

---

25. Further information on this initiative can be obtained from the Critical Infrastructure Assurance Office (CIAO). The National Plan for Information Systems Protection can be viewed at http://www.ciao.gov/National_Plan/national_plan%20_final.pdf. Also of note, programs already exist for the private sector (e.g., the Continuing Education division at the University of Maryland, Baltimore County, which provides a corporate information security curriculum).

26. Many of these legal areas also concern controversial technologies currently employed by law enforcement, such as the FBI's "Carnivore" electronic wiretap system, which allows the FBI to scan ISP servers to access online files of suspected criminals.

■ *Promote transnational cooperation*, within acceptable limits, in addressing attribution of attacks, and subsequent potential retribution, in order not to compromise the national interests of a country that is merely a way point in an attack.

Many countries already have in place very specific definitions and laws concerning cyber crimes. These laws can help deter, prosecute, and sentence perpetrators. They also can help establish a common international definition of cyber crimes, paving the way for more coherent international policies. Of note, the Council of Europe Cybercrime Convention is progressing toward its conclusion. According to the council, its draft cybercrime treaty "will be the first-ever international treaty to address criminal law and procedural aspects of various types of criminal behaviour directed against computer systems, networks or data and other types of similar misuse."[27] The draft treaty was updated at the plenary meeting of the Council of Europe's principal cyber committee in December 2000. It has been submitted to the Parliamentary Assembly for comment (anticipated in April 2001) and will be revised by the European Committee on Crime Problems in June 2001. The treaty will then be ready for adoption by the ministers. Not surprisingly, the ambitious treaty has caused concern among U.S. commercial and libertarian circles because of certain arguably overly restrictive sections (in particular, article 6) and the establishment of costly—sometimes prohibitive—requirements that would be imposed on shared infrastructures as well as on U.S.-controlled assets.[28]

Agreements between nations will of necessity stretch beyond the issues of crime, terrorism, or warfare. Recently, French courts raised a significant and compelling argument that has spurred debate on transnational regulation of the Internet. The French courts asked Yahoo! Inc., to block French viewers from visiting areas of its auction sites that sell Nazi memorabilia. Although Yahoo! is a United States-based company and this request runs against U.S. free speech principles, it is validated by French anti-racist and anti-hate-crime laws that prohibit the sale of such artifacts in France. The court decision treads on the uncharted territory of enforcing national laws through global online services. Once again, the problem is not one of technology. Firms such as Quova, Inc., provide software that will readily identify different user nationalities with 90 percent certainty. France has set an interesting (some might say disturbing) precedent for zoning and regulation of the

---

27. Statement posted on the Council of Europe's Web site, http://conventions.coe.int/. Regular updates on the Draft Convention on Cybercrime are posted on the "Draft Treaties" page.

28. The Council of Europe's cybercrime treaty endeavors to harmonize cybercrime laws and make it easier to prosecute cybercriminals through increased global cooperation. The United States is an observer at the treaty talks. U.S. industry has been particularly concerned with one treaty provision that would require Internet service providers (ISPs) to retain all data traveling over their networks for a period of time. Enacting this measure, however, would be not only costly but also technically impossible, as data volumes continue to increase dramatically. (They are projected to increase one millionfold by 2010.) Similarly, article 6 of the treaty would ban possession of malicious or harmful code. Although the intent of this article is focused on hackers and crackers, this same code is of necessity used by information security providers so a special exception would be needed for such organizations in order for article 6 to be viable. (Paragraph 2 of article 6 attempts to provide such an exception.)

Internet and for providing courts with the authority to impose sanctions outside of their normal jurisdictions.[29] Cases such as these stress the pressing need for clear, agreed-on international standards governing jurisdictional issues.

In establishing international conventions and treaties, it would be useful to examine existing models for international collaboration concerning safety. For example, the norms—such as insurance—established in civil aviation encourage the development of standards that are often initiated by larger economic powers and are adopted by smaller nations because they include guarantees of technical aid and support. In models such as these, certain levels of cooperation become automatic, and information is shared transnationally without violating any nation's sovereignty and without breaching any form of intelligence secrecy.

---

29. For further analysis of the French decision, its international ramifications, and the U.S. reaction, see Sebastian Mallaby, "Le Net, C'est Moi," *Washington Post,* November 27, 2000, p. A21, as well as "Vive La Liberté!" *The Economist,* November 25, 2000, p. 75.

# CHAPTER 7

# Conclusion and Integration of Recommendations

Information technologies will continue to grow and evolve at a staggering pace, infuse themselves into daily activities, and pose adaptation challenges to public and private entities alike, from the global to the local level. Emergent networks such as the Next Generation Internet—the always-on, broadband connection projected to link close to two billion people—not only will create new security conundrums; they will also challenge conventional modes of government intervention such as taxation and regulation. Existing technologies such as open source software already are pushing the boundaries of what existing models of power can realistically control. The ARPAnet (the predecessor to the Internet) was never designed to be secure—and, as one of its architects, Vint Cerf, recently pointed out, security remains inconvenient. The question becomes how much inconvenience is tolerable when U.S. assets are vulnerable and when national security considerations are at stake.

As more complex areas of science such as nanotechnology continue to increase in sophistication, and as elements of chemistry, physics, and biology become increasingly integrated with information technology, the issues of authority, responsibility, and capability to counter cyber threats will be magnified both in scope and in complexity. The need for the government to clearly articulate the problem, its response policy, and a chain of command for both day-to-day activities and times of crisis will remain at the forefront of government's obligations to its individual agencies, the private sector, U.S. citizens, and the international community. To meet these requirements, the government will need to evolve its outlook to a "next generation" focus and to perform thorough, informed, rolling net technological assessments of the state of the art in offensive versus defensive technologies. These assessments should focus on a realistic 5-year time line but should not refrain from speculating and projecting 10 and 20 years out, with the assistance of scenario builders, futurists, and expert researchers pulled in from well beyond the confines of government agencies.

As both the level of "noise" and the sophistication of information weapons increase, the need for rapid reaction will continue to supersede the capability for detection, identification, and prosecution. The United States government must work toward a comprehensive active response policy designed to thwart all forms of anonymous attack on national infrastructures and assets—be they within or outside of U.S. borders—in order to have the necessary flexibility and preparedness to counter the increasing variety of cyber threats effectively and to retaliate in a timely fashion against attackers of unknown origin. The government will not be able to accomplish this goal without the assistance of the private sector. It will be critical for public-sector agencies to continue improving and expanding models for information sharing, education and training, coordination across agencies and sectors, and incentives for improved security both within and outside government.

Only with this caliber of astute investment in intellectual capital, resources, and personnel will the U.S. government truly find itself able to prevent, address, counter, and retaliate against the cyber threats of the future.